Basketball's Third Element:

Improvisation

Volume III

Ron Ekker

ISBN:1492816922
ISBN-13:9781492816928

Thanks to my wife, Ginger, for her endearing support in all my efforts and her tireless work in editing and formatting this book.

TABLE OF CONTENTS

AN INTRODUCTION TO

VOLUME III

Volume III is a manual for coaches and player training. It takes the theory in Volume I and the bridge between theory and application in Volume II, and progresses to the application. In Volume III we discuss the nuts and bolts of a system. It takes a step-by-step approach to offense and defense. All the drills that relate to the system are diagramed and explained. The rules in both the offensive and defensive plans are given. This Volume ends with practice planning and offers the first twelve practice plans for developing the Monk System. Volume III brings closure to the entire theory and application. Good Luck!

CHAPTER TEN

MONK OFFENSE

Where observation is concerned,
chance favors only the prepared mind.

Louis Pasteur

The Monk offense is the core of the Monk system and cannot be replaced, altered, or omitted from the system. It is essential to everything this system of play and training depends on; it is the beat that the system marches to. When this offense is properly taught and internalized, it becomes the foundation for the training of improvisation and instinctive play.

Sufficient information has been shown that playing in the third element is a powerful part of an offensive system. The third element requires improvisation, and the Monk offense fulfils this need because it trains players how to improvise.

The Monk offense has a two-fold function: First, it can be used as a half court offense like a set play. Second—the most important—it is used after a breakdown of a fast break or play because it flows easily and effectively to a sustained attack. It is advisable to use it both ways.

When introducing this offense the initial instruction should be in a half court set-up. It provides the best format for learning the rules of the offense and how to play using the rules. Once mastered in this format, using it in the spaces is easier. There are three major situations when this offense is used to sustain an attack: after a fast break, after a play breakdown, and when no-play is used. Chapter Two verifies that these spaces happen an average of 55.9 times.

The time available in each situation varies. Generally, after a fast break there will be about 18 seconds; after a play breakdown 10-12 seconds; and the time in no-play can be as much as 20 seconds and as little as 3 seconds. It is an important factor that when these spaces occur the defense is not set; they are in scramble. This gives the offense a great advantage. By teaching and practicing the Monk offense, the team will have an attack for these spaces.

The Monk offense is not particularly pretty. What it does very effectively is to produce easy, uncontested shots, almost magically. It does demand sustained movement and this can be a small problem for some players, as it requires an expenditure of energy; some players find that difficult. That is what a coach is for, to demand that players sustain this movement.

Keep in mind that this is a freelance offense. It is not to be confused with the terms *passing game* or *motion*. The passing game, developed on the west coast, relies on a lot of passes and cutting; the term motion most of the time is a play with movement. Freelance is improvisation; the art of making things up without any plan.

The best place to start our explanation of the Monk offense is with the rules. These rules are outlined on the next page, followed by a detailed explanation of each rule.

MONK OFFENSE RULES

AWAY FROM THE BALL:

- Screen—Down, Away, Back-pick.
- Cut—To the basket, to the ball, to the post-up; without screen or with screen
- Fill—provide a passing lane for man with ball or to keep spacing.
- Clear—Clear an area for drive or cut.

WITH THE BALL:

- Shot—Look immediately for shot, if not there look for
- Drive—To basket or for a jump shot, if not there look for
- Pass—first look for pass to cutters, then perimeter pass.

GENERAL RULES:

- Hold ball for 3 counts before passing; give cuts a chance.
- Screener always moves after cut off of screen (Post up, Pops, etc).
- Perimeter spacing is 15-18 feet apart.
- If you are not posting you are perimeter players.

AUTOMATICS: (MUST DO)

- After pass: cut, screen, or fill
- Low post, High Post: 3 counts then <u>must</u> move out.
- If on the weak side spaced at least 15' from lane.
- If overplayed cut to basket then fill or screen.
- On any shot 2-3-4-5 rebounds, 1 protects.

DON'TS: (CAN'T DO)

- Don't screen at the ball
- Don't go behind the man with the ball.

EXPLANATION OF MONK OFFENSE RULES

Away from the Ball

SCREENING

The players look for opportunities to screen for teammates. We use a different style of screening in this offense. It is a screen, not a block. The purpose is only to delay the defensive player; it is up to the cutter to make the right cut. We believe cuts are what make this offense effective and the traditional head hunter screens slow down cuts. They also allow the defense to play very physical which makes running the offense difficult. The quickness of our screening resolves this.

CUTS

These are the backbone of the Monk offense. In the diagrams that follow we show the cuts possible from different positions on the floor. These are cuts without the screen and should be encouraged. The cut from the top is especially important because it demands that the defense adjust, which results in defensive scramble.

When cuts are made with a screen we want the cutter to know how to cut in each type of screen. On a back screen the cutter should walk his defensive man into the screen, and then cut; on the Down Screen and the Side Screen the cutter freezes the defensive player until the screen is set and then cuts.

FILL

This is a passive maneuver but important to team play. It is recognizing and providing a passing lane for a player with the ball. It is also used to keep perimeter spacing. Coaches should pay attention to the weak side perimeter player as they tend to creep towards the basket which clogs up the middle.

CLEAR

By clear we mean to clear out the path of a driver or a cutter. This should

4

be obvious but it does require training. It takes awareness of what teammates are doing. A player may clear in any direction that will provide the driver or cutter an open lane.

With the Ball

SHOT

When a player receives the ball he should look immediately to see if he has a good uncontested shot. If the shot isn't there right away, it won't be there. Players need to be ready to take a shot, but not necessarily to shoot it. If a shot is not available the player should look to drive.

DRIVE

One of the opportunities created by the unpredictable movement of the Monk offense is the drive. It is an important part of the offense. The drive all the way to the basket is preferred, but if it isn't available the drive for a pull-up jump shot is a very good shot. The pull-up jump shot is better than the runner which is a very low percentage shot for most players. If a drive is not available, then look to pass.

PASS

The shot and the drive are available quickly and only for a short time, however if these two are not available the player should look for the pass. He must look into the defense for cutters which is basically the basket area. This offense is unpredictable so the cutters are not defined. A passer must be alert. If the pass into a cutter is not available they use a perimeter pass to keep the offense moving.

The three possibilities listed above is the correct order of priorities when a player receives the ball in the Monk offense.

General Rules

HOLD THE BALL FOR THREE COUNTS BEFORE PASSING

We are more interested in moving players than moving the ball. Holding the ball for three counts allows a player to see a cutter flash open and get the ball to him. The unpredictability of the offense makes this important. Players tend to get rid of the ball quickly and miss scoring opportunities. Coaches need to demand the use of this rule or there will be a lot of easy shot opportunities missed.

SCREENER MOVES AFTER THE CUT

A screener that moves after the cut may get the best shot. Basically, the screener should move opposite the cut. A lot of times this is a pop motion. Make sure the movement creates space between him and his man. The movement may also be a post up or a quick step in. This movement of the screener adds greatly to the overall unpredictability of the offense and it keeps the screeners man from helping on the cutter.

PERIMETER SPACING

The rule is to keep a distance of 15 to 18 feet from another player and from the basket. This keeps the middle open for drivers and cutters. It is easy to congregate at the lane area and this is counterproductive to the offense.

IF NOT POSTING BE A PERIMETER PLAYER

We use this rule to force players to the outside or the high-post when not posting up in the lane. Many players are reluctant to go outside and play as an outside player. The coach needs to stress moving to the outside after a low-post up position. Encourage players to use the high-post position as well as the low-post. After some time of using this offense we found that our most effective results came after the high-post player had touched the ball. The high-post is an excellent passing, driving and shooting position.

Automatics

The automatics are rules that are mandatory. These and the Don'ts are the only rules that must be followed when certain situations appear.

AFTER A PASS

When a player passes he must make some type of movement even if it is just to fill. Passing and cutting are difficult offensive moves for the defense to control. A passer may also move to screen using the screens detailed.

POST UP COUNT

To discourage the tendency of players to stay in the post up—which makes cutting impossible—they must leave the post-up after 3 counts. They can use any maneuver to get out but we encourage moving out to screen the weak side or at the top.

IF OVERPLAYED CUT TO THE BASKET THEN FILL OR SCREEN

If the defense can overplay pass receivers it slows the offense down. It must be automatic to cut to the basket when overplayed. If they don't receive a pass they look for the other options; such as screening and filling. Do not let players keep maneuvering to get the ball in this situation. The minute a player recognizes overplay, he should cut. It is important to spend time training this.

2-3-4-5 REBOUND ALL MISSED SHOTS; 1 PROTECTS

I feel strongly about aggressive rebounding in this offense. With the defense in scramble they are poorly positioned to rebound and this allows for offensive rebounds which result in easy shots. Just because a player attempts to rebound does not mean they can't get back quickly to control fast breaks.

Don'ts

There are certain things that slow down or prohibit the Monk offense. The following two do that and we do not allow either one.

SCREEN AT BALL

The screen at the ball is a two man play while the rest of the team stands. This slows the offense down and it is better to disallow it.

GOING BEHIND THE MAN WITH THE BALL

A player with the ball must be facing the basket to shoot, drive, and see cutters to the basket area. A teammate going behind him allows his defensive player to bother that player and distract him from accomplishing his options. The coach must train players in practice to avoid going behind the player with the ball.

****

This concludes the explanation of the rules for the Monk Offense. Use of these rules is a major challenge for the coach in two ways: First the coach himself must have a clear understanding of the rules and how they are applied; and secondly an equal understanding of how to impart them to the players so they will automatically use them in game conditions. The next chapter focuses on the teaching concepts for this offense.

CHAPTER ELEVEN

TEACHING CONCEPTS FOR THE MONK OFFENSE

*The instructor's business is not to show the way
itself, but to enable the pupil to get the feel of this way
to the goal by adapting it to his individual peculiarities.*

Zen in the Art of Archery
Eugen Herrigel

The Japanese fencing master sometimes uses the Zen method of training. Once, when a disciple came to a master to be disciplined in the art of fencing, the master, who was in retirement in his mountain hut, agreed to undertake the task. The pupil was made to help him gather wood for kindling, draw from the nearby spring, split wood, make the fire, cook rice, sweep the rooms and the garden, and generally look after his household affairs. There was no regular or technical teaching in the art. After some time the young man became dissatisfied, for he had not come to work as servant to the old gentleman, but to learn the art of swordsmanship. So one day he approached the master and asked him to teach him. The master agreed. The result was that the young man could not do any piece of work with any feeling of safety. For when he began to cook rice early in the morning, the master would appear and strike him from behind with a stick. When he was in the midst of his sweeping, he would be feeling the same blow from somewhere, from an unknown direction. He had no peace of mind, he had to be always on the qui vive. Some years passed before he could successfully dodge the blow from whatever source it might come. But the master was not quite satisfied with him yet. One day the master was found cooking his own vegetables over an open fire. The pupil took it into his head to avail himself of this opportunity. Taking up his big stick, he let it fall on the head of the master, who was then stooping over the cooking pan to stir its contents. But the pupil's stick was caught by the master with the cover of the pan. This opened the pupil's mind to the secrets of the art, which had hitherto been kept from him. He then for the first time really appreciated the unparalleled kindness of the master.*

*Suzuki, Daisetz Teitaro, Zen Buddhism and Its Influence on Japanese Culture, pp.7,8

Explaining the teaching concepts of the Monk offense is difficult but it is essential for success. It is different because it is not structured. In a structured offense the players have definite routes and movements which are easy to teach and to learn. It is defined and everyone on the team knows what to do and what to expect. Unfortunately, the defense knows also.

In the Monk offense it is just the opposite. There are no definite routes or movements and each player improvises. This takes away the comfort of predictability and players now play in a different setting in which they must be able to develop innovative movement made up "on the fly". They need to play using their instincts and these instincts need to be trained. If this sounds difficult, it is. It is difficult but doable, and once learned it is transferrable to all types of play.

I am sure all of you remember how you learned to ride a bicycle. Your parents, or someone, started by explaining the things that you needed to do which were rules for riding a bike. Can you recall the first few times? Remember how your handle bars were moving all over the place to keep balance? It was hard to remember how to brake and pedal when you were absorbed in all the things you were told.

But, in a few weeks you were whizzing down the street and your handle bars hardly moved, braking was no problem, and you never thought of the rules your parents gave you. You had internalized them, and they were firmly fixed in your unconscious. You no longer needed to think about them.

This is a simple analogy of how to learn the Monk offense. It isn't about the rules; instead it is about the training. In the bike example you went through a period of trial and error. Slowly, through experience, you became better and as you got better you gained confidence *in yourself*. Then you were able to drive your bike without thinking. That is the Key—you didn't need to think about it.

To coach this offense successfully you must train players, through experience, to rely on their instincts. It does not mean, however, to accept slipshod performance without correction. It requires the patience to give players the opportunity for trial and error experience. Instinctive performance cannot be learned in the classroom or by lectures; it is learned by experience through repetition and monitoring (coaching). Coaches need to accept the results of what the players do instead of how they do it. One must give up the obsession with technique and focus on results. *Once a player strives intently for a clear and well defined result, he finds the right technique.*

Another point is this; it may not look pretty. But, when you see the results you will be willing to give up form for content. It is something that you will have to learn to accept, as it may look like you are not coaching at all. You do your coaching in practice, and let the players play the game.

There is another essential element in teaching this type of offense and that is freedom. The players need freedom to try things that may fail. This is part of learning. The coach will be tempted to direct, but when this is done it becomes structure not freedom.

Teaching, then, walks a fine line between instruction and no instruction. It requires pointing out possibilities, insisting on following the rules, constant repetition of the skills, and incessant practice that allows the players to experience it in team play. There are no short cuts. It requires constant and well planned practice. This kind of playing calls for simplicity instead of complexity. Complexity clutters learning because it requires thinking and this impedes development.

There is considerable literature, most of it ancient, which speaks to these learning issues. I would encourage all coaches to spend time reading this literature. To help those who wish to delve deeper into this subject, I would recommend three books. These are: *The Inner Game of Tennis* by W. Timothy Gallwey; *Effortless Mastery* by Kenny Werner, and *Zen in the Art of Archery* by Eugen Herrigel. These books cover three different performance activities (tennis, piano, and archery) other than basketball, but they identify and explain a concept for learning the improvisational style of the Monk offense.

In order for the Monk offense to be effective, the players must have faith in their instincts. For players to develop this faith three things must take place: first, a clear vision of the result desired; second, the opportunity to experience the activity; and third, the activity(s) must be internalized into the unconscious through intense repetition.

The strength of learning through experience rather than teaching, and internalizing this learning through repetition brings about instinctive performance. This type of performance is seamless, effortless, quick, and effective.

Personally, I believe that this instinctive style of play cannot fail. Also, I believe that if a player or players cannot play this way, it will keep them from success at a higher level. I commend the coach that has the courage and the will to help players learn in this way—not only for basketball, for life.

CHAPTER TWELVE

PRESENTING THE MONK OFFENSE

Whoso would be a man must be an nonconformist.

Self-Reliance
Ralph Waldo Emerson

The content in this chapter discourages many coaches from this type of offense because it is difficult to coordinate a team of five players that results in a unified effort, without set plays. It means coaching at a new and different level. A coach must be patient, accommodating, firm, disciplined, confidant, and committed. Success is slow to realize, but if the effort is sustained until excellence is reached the results can be outstanding.

It is important that you are convinced this is a better way. Furthermore, you must be willing to put in the time and effort to study how the mind and the body are one. Chapter Four detailed the use and importance of instinctive and improvisational play and training. Training players in this style requires commitment on the part of the coach. This chapter will assist the coach not acquainted with a free lance offense.

I believe the introduction of this offense, or any other, should be at the team level and not at the drill level. This is the whole, part method of teaching. Show them the whole first, and then develop the parts. It is helpful for the players to see the whole offense first, and then the parts become more meaningful. Thus show the Monk offense first as a set half-court offense.

Start with the set-up shown in Frame 1; a two guard front, two wings high, and a high post.

High Post Half Court Set

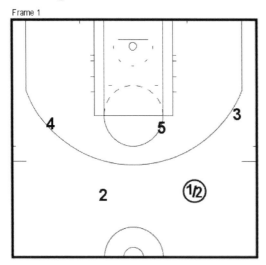

Demonstrate the initial positions. The high post man is always at the elbow on the side of the ball. The two guard front allows for a guard to guard pass making it easy to enter either side. The two guards should be spread the distance of the lane lines as shown. The wings start low and break to the positions shown in this diagram. These positions evaporate quickly but it is helpful to establish a starting point when this offense is taught and when used as a half-court offense in games.

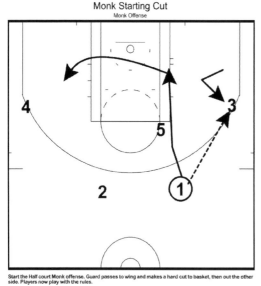

Monk Starting Cut
Monk Offense

Start the Half court Monk offense. Guard passes to wing and makes a hard cut to basket, then out the other side. Players now play with the rules.

Next, demonstrate the guard to wing pass and the cut by the passer as shown in this Frame. This cut is essential because it is difficult to defend, and the defense has to make an adjustment to protect against a layup by the cutter.

Usually this will force them into scramble. When the Monk offense is used as a half-court set, this pass and cut starts the offense. After this cut the players can do anything they want within the rules. The players are now in control and whatever they choose to do, within the rules, is right. I am sure the last two sentences will cause most coaches to shudder. Have courage and give it a chance.

The coach now explains the rules, carefully making generous use of demonstrations. Don't assume--explain and demonstrate. Allow plenty of time and take the time. If you hand out the rules to the players, don't assume they will read them. You should teach like they have never seen them. Personally, I do not hand out the rules at this time.

That is the easy part, next is the hard part. Split the team into groups of five (or six) players, and each group should have a ball. Put one team on the floor without defense. The guards start at the timeline and bring the ball into the starting position. They must make the pass to the wing followed by the cut. This pass and cut must take place before the offense can be run; be a stickler on this and make the pass be a good one and then a good cut. The coach's focus is now on acquainting the players with the rules. Do not expect the players to know what they are doing. It takes time as steps of progression must be taken. Carefully make corrections of the use of the rules and make suggestions of possibilities that the players may try. Be careful that the players understand suggestions are only possibilities and not directives.

The temptation is to split the team into groups—each group working at a different basket--so that more repetitions are possible. <u>Please do not do this</u>. Keep all the players together and have each group rotate after one possession. You want all the players to get the same instructions from the same voice. This method is a little slower, but it is more effective.

After ample practice without defense—maybe a few practices-- add a defensive team. Always rotate teams equally after each possession so they all get equal time. Using offense to defense, and defense to offense after each possession is effective with two teams. If there are three teams, use offense to defense; defense out, new team on offense. This works nicely.

The offense will look terrible. The players will be confused and completely disregard or forget the rules. They will not know how to create opportunities. The coach must patiently instruct, encourage, and correct. The players may start to direct each other. They are making plays. You have to stop this. Be careful, as a coach that you don't make plays—point out possibilities not directives. Each possession will be different, and should be. The first few days it is best to focus on learning the rules.

Eventually, the Monk offense is broken down into team drills that teach the players all the skills they will need to run the offense smoothly. As the drills are introduced and mastered, the offense begins to take life. But, even in the rough beginning you will notice that open uncontested shots appear almost magically out of nowhere.

After the first day slowly begin to inject the breakdown drills that are diagramed and explained in succeeding chapters. The sequence listed below is the order that I found to be effective:

1. Monk cuts: this is the most important and effective skill in the offense. It should be mastered first.
2. Screen Away Cuts: this helps to get the weak side players involved but don't fall in love with it as it is not one of the better offensive situations, but it is a good training drill.
3. Screen down Cuts: It takes some time for players to be able to use all of the stunts effectively, so allow time to teach this drill because mastery will come slowly. This is an important drill in the Monk offense.
4. Split Cuts: Players forget to throw to a post-up man, and then to split. This drill will help that.
5. Back Screen Cuts: Players will see and want to use this more but it has limited effectiveness so wait to work on it.
6. Baseline Screen Cuts: I would not hurry to use this drill but players should be encouraged to be aware of this cut it in team play.

Add drills slowly. It is best to develop some degree of mastery in each drill before adding another. Do not short cut repetition—it is essential. You will learn, if you are serious, how to use and alternate these drills. I have never found it necessary to run any other drills because in teaching, less is better than more. Strive for simplicity and excellence.

The players should work on Monk everyday with and without defense. This is where players will get comfortable with using the skills that are involved in team play.

CHAPTER THIRTEEN

MONK OFFENSE PREPARATION

In the Monk system a drill is a physical or mental exercise aimed at perfecting ease in performance of the team (whole). The term drill suggests perfection of a specific skill, but not necessarily relating to the whole and this is self-defeating. Practice that does not strive to make total performance better is unnecessary and is not preparation. Practicing unnecessary activities is wasting time and energy. In the Monk system practice is designed and implemented to drive team performance to a higher level.

Drills, then, must relate directly to the performance desired in a game. The coach must be relentless in scrutinizing each practice activity to determine if that activity meets the standard of relating directly to the whole team performance.

We have a term for developing team related skills. They are called *breakdown drills* and should not be confused with the term play breakdown. Breakdown drills will isolate important parts of team offense, team defense, and the third element for selective practice.

It is important to do breakdown drills daily. It's not necessary to do many, but to work your way through these drills in some type of order to insure that all are mastered. In the previous chapter a priority order of the breakdown drills was provided. Once these drills are thoroughly learned they require only a small amount of practice time to maintain mastery.

The breakdown drills for the Monk Offense are presented in the next chapter but this chapter will describe and explain some team drills. They are: 3 on 3; 4 on 4; and 5 on 5. These give the players excellent practice in team coordination, and learning to create within the team concept. They are explained in the next few pages.

3 on 3:

In 3 versus 3 players are put into situations that require unpredictable improvisation which helps to develop this skill. The more you use it the more creative players will become. I used the big players as perimeter players in this drill--but not more than one big in each group of three. Each group of three should have smalls (1-2-3) and bigs (4-5) so that each group is balanced. It is best to change groups each day so players learn to play with all of their teammates. This is wonderful preparation but requires some coaching skill and the players should first have a good foundation in the use of the rules.

At first the players will not know what to do and will appear clumsy. Let them work through it on their own as much as you can but make sure they are using the rules. A good way to teach is to wait until a situation occurs, then explain and demonstrate possibilities. These situations will occur if you have patience and are alert to recognize them. At times, I have shown something like Frame 2, but you should be careful as the players may fall in love with it and use it like a play.

Encourage players at all times to use innovative creation. Keep the team together for this drill so the players can learn from observation what other players are doing, and can hear the instruction. The players will accidentally find a lot of interesting situations. Be alert to point these out in an encouraging voice. Because of the limited number of players, filling (see the rules for definition) is essential and this drill will help to make it automatic in game conditions. Because 3 versus 3 is wide open it provides opportunities for drives. This builds confidence in the player's ability to use them.

Lastly, it is a great defensive drill. The defense should use the ball line defense rules. They will need to be very good to stop the offense in this drill because there is very little off the ball help and this will force them to be effective in playing the ball, contesting shots, and rebounding.

Though I explain this drill first in this discussion, it should be introduced last. The players need the background of understanding the rules and team play learned in 5 versus 5, and 4 versus 4, before they can handle this drill.

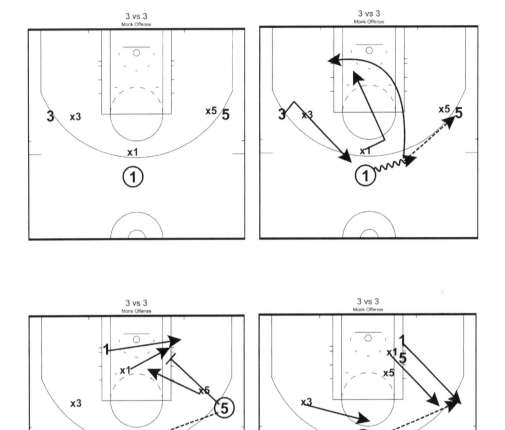

Frame 1(Frames are from left to right) shows the starting positions for 3 versus 3; Frame 2: 1 passes to 5 and makes the cut to the basket and 3 Fills from the weak side; Frame 3: 1 cuts back to strong-side post up, 5 recognizes this and passes to 3 at the top and 5 goes to set a screen-down for 1; 1 uses screen to cut to wing, at this time 1 has all the ball options, 5 can post-up and 3 could cut or go away.

Remember, that this is just a possibility. Players should be discouraged from using this like a play, and rely on innovative play instead.

The coach's ability to watch both the offense and the defense is a factor. It can be done successfully, but it does take some experience. If you have trouble with this and have an assistant put him in charge of watching the defense only. Most coaches will focus on the offense and the defense gets shoddy. This creates bad habits that will show up in a game. A coach must be diligent and not allow this, even though this is an offensive drill.

4 on 4 Drill:

This is an important drill for learning the Monk Offense. I used it almost every day, and all season long. It gives the coach a chance to help players see opportunities. There is more space available than in 5 on 5, which makes it easier to see the possibilities and to point out mistakes. It is also excellent for learning the ball line defense.

As this drill is introduced coaches should be aware of rhythm. Make a point to the players not to hurry, and allow things to happen. Frantic players make mistakes and miss opportunities. The rule which states to hold the ball for 3 counts needs to be emphasized in this drill. Allow players to find their own pace or rhythm, and don't force your perception of how fast they should play. Don't allow sloth, but don't force speed either. Rhythm includes timing and it is an intricate balance to teach and to learn but it must be done because good execution cannot be attained without it.

This is also a good drill for teaching shot selection. This drill will provide shot opportunities. Be alert to point out faulty shot selection. A coach should know what shots he wants and which shots are appropriate for a specific player.

Try not to have too many similar players on each group of 4. Don't overload one position.

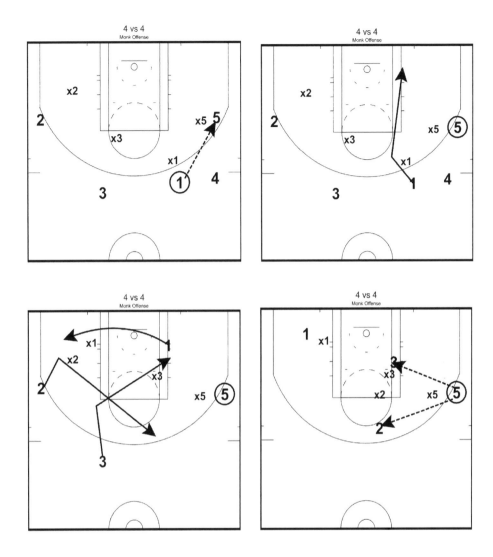

Frame 1 (Frames are from left to right) shows the starting positions and the guard to wing pass. Frame 2 shows the essential cut. The Frames 3 and 4 show a possibility only. After the Monk cut, it becomes free-lance with the use of the rules.

The possibilities in this drill are limitless and it puts great pressure on the defense because everything is unpredictable. Make sure the players on offense don't get stuck doing only one thing. This happens a lot. Be quick to spot this, but use discretion in correcting it.

5 on 5 Drill:

I used 5 on 5 to introduce the Monk offense; the two preceding drills (3 on 3, and 4 on 4) are the building blocks for it. In 5 on 5 always start in the original Monk set-up: 2 guard front, 2 wings high, and a High post man. It starts, always, with a wing pass and a cut to the basket. After that cut, the positions disappear and creativity takes place.

When teaching the complete offense I keep the team at half-court and rotate teams. Of course, we did scrimmage full-court, but in the teaching and learning period we stayed half-court.

During the half-court play, we eventually begin to use a shot clock. This gives the players a chance to learn about time and to build an inner clock of their own. Players can get a good a sense of the time left without seeing the shot clock.

In the middle of the season, and with players more comfortable with the offense, we would add situations to 5 on 5. For example, I may make them play without dribbling. Occasionally, I would designate a certain player to get a shot. Now the team would have to keep working until that player got open and the team found him. I may designate a certain shot, such as a layup, post up, jump shot, or drive. Also, I will combine the last two, and the team would have to get a certain player a specific shot. They are playing at a high level when they can do that.

There is no diagram for 5 on 5 as we have already diagramed the half-court Monk offense set up.

Half Court Full Court Play:

To give the players the sense of running the Monk offense from a full-court situation I used a controlled scrimmage. Team A starts with the ball in the half-court and runs Monk. Team B is on defense. When Team A gives up the ball, regardless of how (Made FG, Def Rebound, Steal, and Turnover), Team B responds immediately with a fast break, or push, or walk up. Team A changes to defense. Team B continues until they give up the ball. But after a full-court Team B keeps the ball and they run a half-court Monk with Team A on defense. When Team B gives up the ball in their half-court Team A would respond with a full-court offense (fast break, push, walk it up). After their full-court they would keep the ball and start a half-court.

Each team has a half-court opportunity and a full-court opportunity. Remember to stop play after a full-court opportunity, and give the ball back to the same team so they can run a half-court offense. This can get confusing in actual use, so the coach may want to assign someone to keep track of what the situation is. One situation is difficult to manage: When a team receives the ball after a made basket and they walk the ball up and run a half-court offense—even though this is called a full court possession and when it ends that team still has another half-court to do.

This drill gives the coaches and players some control. There are breaks in the play when instruction can take place. I found this to be extremely helpful in working on all aspects of our offense and defense.

When I put in our Set Offense we continued to use this drill with that offense also. Now our team was beginning to see and use Monk in the spaces also. Specifically when converting to the Monk offense after a fast break attempt, and after a play breakdown. This drill is a very important part of preparing our team for scrimmage and games.

I felt with this half-court, full-court set up, the team was working on everything we needed in a game. I could organize it anyway I wanted which allowed us to work on Monk, Sets or any other part of our offense and defense. It works very well with 4 on 4 also.

SUMMARY

This concludes the explanation of the Monk Offense. It is shown, so far, as a half court offense. I think it is important to introduce it first as a half-court offense. It is the best way to learn the rules, master the skills, and incorporate all this into a team concept. It also brings into play group improvisation.

Coaches will find using Monk as a half-court offense in games will strengthen its development. They may find out, as I did, at times it is their best half-court offense. It is especially helpful when a team plays a lot of games against the same opponent, such as in the playoffs. In that situation the opponents learn your plays very well and can prepare for them. Monk is unpredictable, so they cannot prepare for it. For me it solved a lot of problems in the playoffs. In one game in particular, we ran it almost the whole game to win our series.

It has two uses: as a half-court offense, and as an organized attack to take advantage of play in the spaces. In this way it can easily be used 30 to 40 times in a game. It can be an integral part of a team's offensive repertoire. We will go into more detail in its use as a scramble offense in future chapters.

Monk is a concept of unpredictable movement. I believe, though, that a complimentary set offense is mandatory. I would not encourage the use of Monk exclusively, as it is demanding physically and mentally. It requires a high degree of concentration which is necessary for creativeness and improvisation.

I always taught the Monk Offense first and then the set offense. There are a couple of reasons. First, the individual skills learned in Monk are the same skills that are needed in any set offense, with the exception of the screen and roll. This makes the set offense more effective and compliments the teaching. Secondly, having the Monk offense in place allows it to be used in the spaces. Normally, we allowed about 5 to 6 practices before we went to the set offense. However, this was with college or professional players. For less experienced players it will take longer in the Monk offense to obtain the mastery necessary before advancing to the set offense.

There is one more remark about the Monk Offense. It will change your players in their basketball development and as a person. It forces them to learn valuable long term skills such as moving without the ball, high percentage shot selection, importance of working within a team concept, and enhancement of their basketball intelligence. It helps to make them better all-around players. It will also change you, the coach. You will reach a deeper understanding of the game of basketball.

CHAPTER FOURTEEN

MONK OFFENSE SKILLS AND DRILLS

The wrapping does not make the gift you give. An empty box, however beautiful and gently given, still contains nothing.

The Course in Miracles, pp. 495

In teaching the Monk offense, it is necessary to introduce breakdown drills so players will learn how to execute easily and instinctively under game conditions. However, none of these drills will have the results desired unless they are taught correctly and repeated continuously. It is best to work with just a few drills. Excessive drills just clutter the players learning experience. The purpose is to become so acquainted with the mechanics of each drill that the players focus on performance of the skill set rather than the complexity of the drill. The reason for this simplicity and repetition is to internalize the skills so they can execute them instinctively and automatically.

SKILL SETS

In the Monk system each of the breakdown drills has a specific purpose that relates directly to the team offense and the team's mission. In most cases rather than an individual skill, each drill will be a *skill set*. A skill set is a single team skill with multiple options. For example, the Screen Down employs five cuts by the cutter and five moves by the screener. In relation to the team offense, the Screen Down is just a single team skill; the options within the Screen Down make it a set of skills, thus it is termed a *skill set*. Most of the breakdown drills in the Monk system are a skill set. They relate directly to the whole which is an important concept of the Monk system.

In this chapter diagrams are provided with explanations of the drills. Each set of diagrams shows the skill and the drill used to master the skill or skill set.

These drills may seem simple. Coaches tend to be attracted to complex and flashy drills, many times to show off their teaching skills. The question is, are the players learning? The drills in the Monk system are not designed to entertain or look good, they are meant to facilitate learning. They provide the repetition that is necessary for instinctive execution under game conditions. Each drill is simple to help the players get proficient in using it.

TEACHING THE MONK DRILLS

These drills do not need to be run for long periods of time. The emphasis is on execution and progress. Use shorter times and repeat consistently. When the drill is being run correctly, move on to the next one. Don't let it become laborious. Through experience the coach will learn the number of times and the time required for each drill; but do not short change excellence.

I have two warnings about teaching drills. First, don't tweak the drill to make it more interesting. Each drill has a specific purpose and changing the drill, even slightly, weakens that purpose. These drills are developing and internalizing a certain skill or skill set, so keep the emphasis on that.

Secondly, don't let yourself become bored with the drill. You must stay involved mentally. Do not let it get sloppy even if it has been run for months. It is the coach's responsibility to make players use these drills regularly to reach a high level of expertise. In the Monk system, good is the minimum standard desired but that is not what we strive for. We strive for excellence.

Monk Cuts:

It is best to start by teaching cuts as they are the backbone of the Monk Offense. The diagrams that follow show the cuts from different positions on the floor. These positions are not exactly like in a game, because in this offense there are no exact positions. The drills give the angles and distances that are similar to what is used in games. It is necessary to use the drills regularly so that players get comfortable with the angles, the distances, and the use of the cuts. Defense may be added after the cuts are internalized but not before. Be patient.

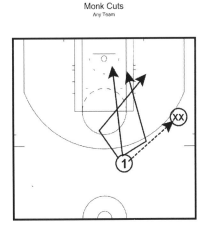

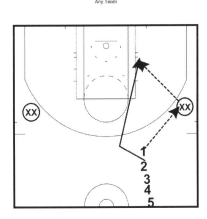

These are the cuts from the top. XX is a coach. I prefer a coach do the passing so good passes are made to each player on the cuts. Players form a line as shown in the diagram on the right. Three balls should be used in this drill. Players pass and cut for the lay-up, retrieve their ball and pass to the next player in line and go to end of the line. Use the drill on both sides. Players should be taught to take a jab step in the opposite direction and drive hard off of their outside leg to make the cut to the basket.

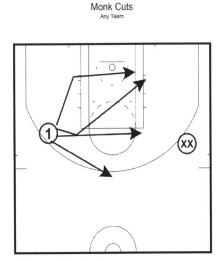

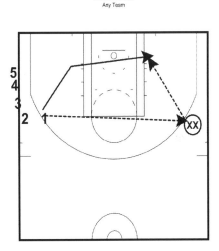

Diagram on the left shows the potential cuts that can be made from the weak-side. Coach is in the position shown. The players are in line with three balls. First player throws cross court to the coach and uses one of the cuts for a shot; he rebounds the ball and throws to next in line, and goes to the end of the line. These weak-side cuts should be used from both sides.

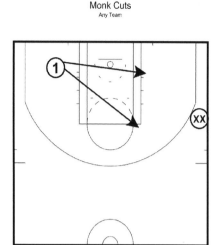

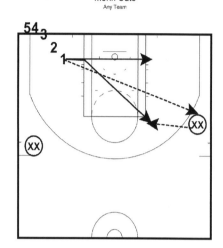

The cuts from a position shown in the diagram at the left are limited but need to be mastered. The drill on the right is similar to other cutting drills. Players line up in positions shown; first three players have a ball, pass to coach and cut to the elbow or low-post for shot, rebound to next person in line, and go to the end of the line.

In teaching cuts—or any skill set drill—it is permissible, and encouraged, to specify the use of one cut only. This is necessary to acquire skill in each one but eventually the players should be given the freedom to make their own selection.

Screen Away Cuts:

The weak-side screen away is not effective under game conditions because the position of the ball makes it easy to defend. But it is a good teaching drill because it incorporates the cuts using a screen, and the moves of the screener. The screener usually comes from the top position. Because it is a side screen the cutter freezes his man until the screen is set and this done by faking a cut to the baseline which sets his man up for the screen from the top. The cutter has five stunts available to him and they are illustrated in the diagrams. Defense can be added to this drill after all players have the cuts internalized and they have become automatic. The cuts and screener moves are basic for all the rest of the screening away from the ball skill sets. So starting with the Screen Away drill prepares players for the rest of the offensive skill sets.

There are a few terms used in this drill that should be explained before we start with the remainder of the drills.

POP: This is a move made by the screener after a certain cut is made, usually a back cut or a curl. In reaction to the cut, the screener steps back, straight back, to separate himself from his defensive player, who many times steps with the cutter to provide help. The screener can get many good shots by using this maneuver.

BACK-CUT: This cut is made when the defensive player anticipates a cut in one direction and plays it aggressively. The cutter fakes the anticipated cut, and then cuts in the opposite direction.

CURL: The cutter starts in one direction off of the screen, but curls around the screen instead. The diagram in this drill will show that clearly.

SLIPPING THE SCREEN: The player screening goes to set the screen, however, just before he gets there he cuts to the basket instead. This is very effective if the defense is zoning the screen, or switching.

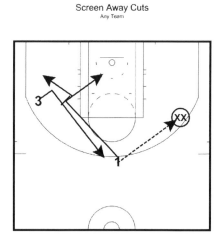
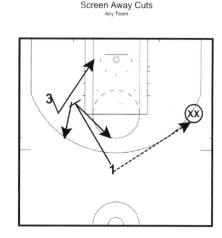

Screen Away Cuts
Any Team

Diagram on the left shows the basic cut in screen away. Player on top passes to coach and sets the screen on weak-side wing. Wing sets up defensive man and cuts to the top of the key, screener rolls or pops. Diagram on right shows the back-cut and the screener *pops* or fills to the top of the key.

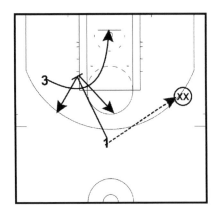
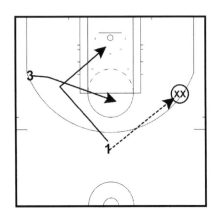

Screen Away Cuts
Any Team

Screen Away Cuts
Any Team

Diagram on the left shows the *curl* cut; the screener pops or fills to the top. On the right is a powerful move by the screener, he *slips the screen* with a cut to the basket. The cutter reacts with a cut to the top of the key to fill.

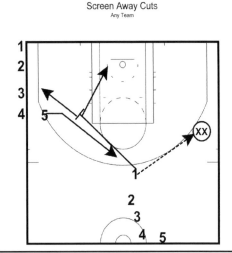

Screen Away Cuts
Any Team

Screen Away Cuts
Any Team

On the left the cutter looks like he is cutting to the top but instead makes a back-door cut, the screener reacts with a pop or a cut to the top of the key. Diagram on the right is the drill used to teach these cuts. It is similar to other drills but with two lines. Three balls in the line at the top of the key. Pass is made to the coach and the players may use any of the cuts, or the designated cut as indicated by the coach. Players change lines after the play. Practice from both sides.

In the Screen Away drill as in all drills the cuts and screening reactions should be demonstrated correctly. It is best to teach one cut at a time, allowing ample time on each to attain some degree of skill. Let the players go slowly at first, then let the drill speed up. Once they have gone through all of the cuts, let them use whichever one they want. When the players are comfortable, encourage the drill to move quickly with the initial pass to the coach starting as soon as the two players in front finish.

Screen Down Cuts:

In the Monk offense there are opportunities for a Screen Down (or Pin Down). This is a generic term that simply means screening a man below the screener. It usually occurs when a wing player passes to a top player, and there is a post-up player or a player on the baseline on the ball side. In a Screen Down, the cutter holds and sets up his man for the screen and then cuts. There are five possible cuts off of this type of screen and all are shown in the diagrams along with the moves by the screener.

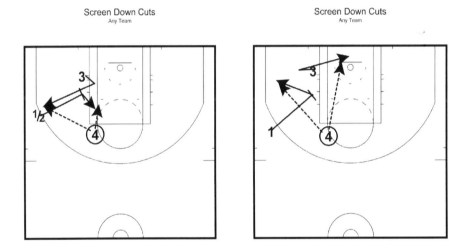

Diagram on the left shows the basic cut on a screen down (or pin down). The cutter (3) sets up his man for the screener, and cuts to the wing. The screener opens first to the passer (4) at the elbow then to the wing man. The passer should be alert to pass to either player. On the right, the cutter uses a back-cut and the screener pops.

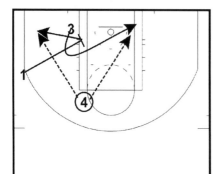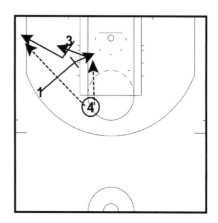

In the left diagram the cutter makes a curl move and the screener pops. In the right one, the cutter flares to the corner and the screener moves to post-up as he did in the first diagram. A flare move is a flat cut rather than an angle cut and is used if the defensive man cuts through on the ball-side of the screener.

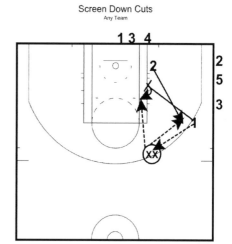

On the left, the cutter uses what we term a baby curl (a variation of the curl, it is not a tight curl but a longer one), and the screener may step into the basket or pop. On the right is the drill used to teach the different maneuvers. There are two lines, one at the wing and one on the baseline. Three balls in the wing line, the wing man passes to the coach and sets the screen for baseline man who uses any cut and the screener reacts to the cut. Coach can pass to either the cutter or the screener for a shot. Players exchange lines after retrieving the ball and pass to the wing line.

The Screen Down is a very important screening situation in the Monk offense. The cuts and screeners moves need to be perfected. Ample practice time should be allotted for this skill set.

One note on this drill and all the drills: *I never use two balls.* This is a cutting drill, not a shooting drill, though the players do get experience in the shots they will get. However, the player that receives the second ball does not get a game like shot; and the second ball just clutters the drill and distracts from the teamwork needed in the skill set.

Split Cuts:

A Split is when two players cross, one being the screener, the other being the cutter. In the Monk offense, anytime the ball is thrown to a low post player it requires a split cut and the player that makes the pass to the post-up is always the screener. To be effective the splits require stunts. All of these stunts are shown and can be used effectively. The post-player with the ball should also look to score. Be diligent in requiring good passes on this drill. Do not let the players get sloppy with their passes.

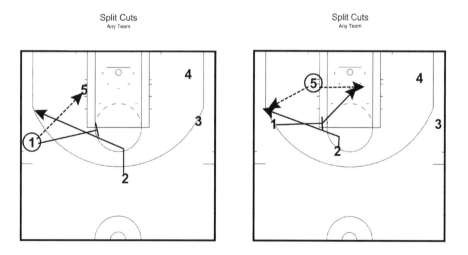

On the left, the wing man passes to the post-up man and moves to set a screen for the top player who in this case cuts over the top of the screen. The right frame shows the cut and movement of the screener, who is using a roll to the basket.

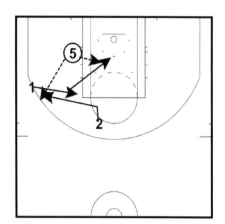

On the left, the top cutter fakes going over the screen and cuts to basket (back-cut), the screener makes the movement shown. On the right, the screener slips the screen (fakes it) and cuts to the basket, and the top man continues over the top.

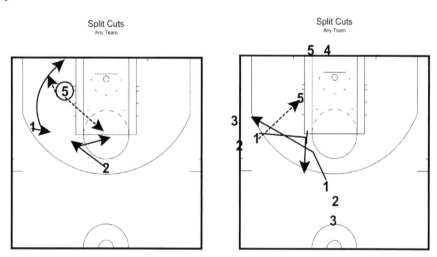

The wing initiates the cuts shown in the left diagram by making a baseline cut after the pass and the top man makes the move shown. On the right is the drill that is used to perfect this skill, one line at the top with three balls, a line of wings, and a line of post-up players. The top man starts the drill passing to the wing that passes to the post-up player, and then the cuts are made. The wing and the top players exchange lines after their turn. The post-up players do not exchange lines but can be rotated to become outside players at the discretion of the coach.

Passing to a post up player followed by the split maneuver is a very effective scoring situation. This allows for improvisation at its highest level. Perfection of these skills will open up a lot of opportunities.

Back Screen Cuts:

This type of screen occurs very naturally in the flow of the Monk offense. It usually occurs when a wing player makes a pass to the player at the top. If there is a player on the baseline or lane line, he can quickly and easily step out for a back screen on the passer's man. The cuts by the cutter and the moves of the screener are diagramed. On a back screen, the cutter must walk his man into the screen and then make the cuts.

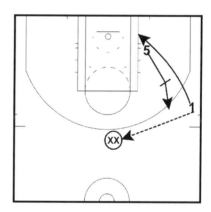

The left diagram shows a typical back screen and cut. After the wing man's pass, the baseline or post-up player steps up to set a stationary screen. The cuts in both diagrams above are similar; one goes over the top and the other goes behind. The screener's moves are the same on both.

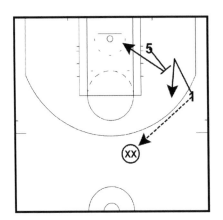

This move is initiated by the cutter and is called a *step-back*. The screener cuts to the basket. The drill is the same as the other drills. Two lines, wing line has three balls, the pass is made to the coach, the screener sets the screen and the cutter cuts, the coach can pass to either one. Players change lines.

The back screen and cut are popular with players and are looked for excessively. Unfortunately, it is attempted many times when the ball is in a bad position for a pass, such as when the screen and cut are on the weak side. Make sure the players understand this.

Baseline Screen Cuts:

The baseline screen usually occurs when a low post player on the ball side, vacates to the weak side. It becomes very effective when it is spontaneous and unpredictable. There are only two cuts available, though there can be some modifications of these cuts. However, any modifications may clutter the screener's moves. I would not use defense in this drill.

On the left, 2 walks his man into the screen and makes a cut on the baseline side to post-up, the screener cuts to the elbow on the ball side. The second option in the diagram on the right is the same except the cutter fakes baseline and cuts to the elbow, the screener cuts to the post up (they exchange roles).

Monk: Baseline Screen Cuts
Any Team

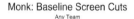

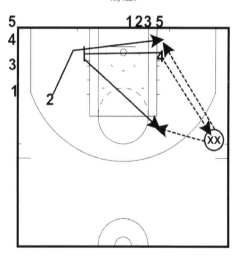

DRILL: Three balls in line on the baseline. Baseline man with the ball passes to the coach, moves to post-up then reverses to the weak side lane line and sets a stationary screen, the wing man walks the defensive man into the screen and makes either cut. The screener reacts accordingly. The coach passes to either man. The players exchange lines.

SUMMARY

These breakdown drills are the basis of the Monk offense, and used judiciously will develop those skills necessary for smooth group improvisation. This will carry over to set plays. *Essentially the Monk offense is an intricate combination of interrelated parts used in freelance.* Though appearing as parts working separately, it becomes, through the use of the rules, interrelated but unpredictable. To accomplish this, cuts and screens must be unified into a cohesive performance.

Avoid using competition during the learning period of the breakdown drills. It is easy for players to become more involved in the competition than the proper execution. Competition can be added as skills are well learned. The same is true about the use of defense. Defense should be added only after execution is perfected. I seldom used defense or competition in these drills; some years I never used defense or competition. I prefer for the players to develop playing against defense in 5 versus 5 practice and games. In drills the defense can easily play the play and this distracts from the learning process, and can destroy the confidence of the player's ability to use these stunts.

CHAPTER FIFTEEN

MONK OFFENSE INDIVIDUAL SKILLS

One person with passion is better than forty who are merely interested.

Inside the Magic Kingdom
Tom Connellan

Shot Selection

Shot selection is the most important skill that is required in the Monk offense. In a rehearsed, but unstructured offense like the Monk, it is difficult to tell which player will end up with the shot. Each player should be taught what a high percentage shot is for him. The players need to learn that if they don't have a high percentage shot, they don't take it unless it is at the end of the shot clock. They keep working until they get the high percentage shot desired. The coach must be clear of the type of shot that can be taken. Training players to understand good shot selection is essential. A coach cannot be slack in this part of training. Bad shot selection must be corrected consistently and at the time it occurs. True field goal percentage usually determines who wins the game. A good field goal percentage is a result of getting and taking the right shots.

Passing

Passing is a poorly trained, but important skill in any type of basketball. In the Monk offense it takes on special importance because player movement is unpredictable. Consequently, each player must be alert to spontaneous openings and have the skill to deliver an accurate pass. This does not require flashy passing as much as sensible passing. In a similar way that muscles atrophy from not being used; passing atrophies from lack of passing. It can be revived and strengthened with proper practice; the best passing practice is in the drills and in team play. Coaches miss on this. They will practice stationary passing drills, and then allow sloppy passing in drills. Insist on good passing in the drills and do not allow it to be sloppy or lackadaisical.

When teaching young or inexperienced players it is appropriate to use stationary drills. However, with the more advanced player this is redundant. The advanced player needs intensity in practice drills and games to acquire the necessary skill.

Cuts or cutting

In offensive basketball cuts are of key importance. The Monk offense specializes in it. Cuts provide more easy baskets than any other offensive maneuver. Teaching the mechanics of cuts is important but learning the when, the where, and the how separates the skilled from the unskilled players. As in all skills, it is necessary for it to become instinctive. This can only be accomplished through practice, repetition, and experience. If you do not provide players with these essentials, it will be done poorly or not at all. Poorly trained players tend to cut indiscriminately and they need to be instructed to make cuts with a purpose.

Driving

This is a basketball term that I cannot assume every person will understand. It occurs when a player can dribble by his defensive man, and is free, or partially free, to go to the basket. The Monk offense, due to its movement, will create many opportunities for drives because it breaks down the support principles of the defense. It is important that players are made aware of these opportunities, and that they have the skill to be effective. Shot selection is also important with this maneuver. Of course, the layup is the premier shot desired, but sometimes it is met with the strongest resistance. The pull up jump shot, at short range, is easier to get uncontested and more effective than the runner (the runner is a shot attempted while movement is at a high speed as in a drive). The players in Monk have to be instructed and practiced in this skill consistently. This is a skill that is best perfected in live play such as in 5 on 5.

Screening and use of Screens

Screens are overrated skills; use of screens is underrated. If a screen fails it is the cutters fault, not the screeners. An acceptable screen does not need to stop a defensive player, just delay him. The cutter is the key. He must position his man correctly, and make the best cut at the right time. Timing and unpredictability make the screen effective.

An important component of the screen is the movement of the screener after the cut. The screener must learn an instinctive and spontaneous move after any type of cut. Nothing helps the cutter more than if the screener's man cannot help due to counter movement by the screener. Coaches put too much emphasis on a screen blocking a defensive man completely, called in some circles a "head hunter screen". These types of screens slow the offense down and restrict its effectiveness. They are not the type of screen desired in the Monk offense.

Rebounding

There is a great deal of emphasis in today's basketball on getting back to stop a fast break, at the expense of the offense getting a high percentage shot from a rebound. Offensive rebounding does not require a lot of skill, but it does require determination and the freedom to pursue rebounds aggressively. This is another area that the Monk offense creates many opportunities. The movement of the offense creates a scramble situation which breaks down the defense's ability to get good rebounding position. Obtaining the proverbial "second shot" is an effective offensive skill that needs to be part of the system.

Shooting

The correct shot selection will take care of most shooting problems, but the players must be comfortable with the shots that they will get in this offense. The players need ample repetition in the type of shots that are produced by the offense. This is not just "getting up shots", but diligent practice in the shots produced in Monk. Almost all shots in a game are the result of some kind of movement, and shooting should be practiced with that movement. There also has to be the determination to create good shots, and avoid accepting only those shots the defense will give you. In the last five minutes of a competitive game the defense will not give you shots you can make--the offense must create them.

****

This brings us to the next chapter which deals with a set offense. It is an offense that I have used successfully and fits well with the Monk concept. The skills learned and perfected in the Monk offense enhance dramatically the set offense.

CHAPTER SIXTEEN

HALF COURT SET OFFENSE: CUT

Improvising on the Play

I enjoy giving books to people, but I never give a book that I have not read and found worthwhile. In the same way, I would not suggest a half-court offense that I have not used successfully. The set offense that I describe in this book is an offense that has been successful and it is a good compliment to Monk. It involves similar movement and freedom.

The name of this set offense is *Cut*. It provides movement, unpredictability, and simplicity. There is, however, one important part that has some degree of complexity. That part will be pointed out in the explanation.

Along with our explanation, there are diagrams that will help to clarify its design and execution. We show only Cut, Cut 2 and Automatic. As the players learned the sets, we incorporated some other options, but they are not included in this book. These three sets, along with Monk, comprise a substantial offense and provide everything that is needed.

CUT

Cut is a simple offense but appears complex to the opponents. The initial positions are 2 guards, 2 wings, and a high post. This is, of course, the same initial set up as Monk. I feel that having them look alike is an advantage. The entry pass to the wing, and the cut by the guard is the same as in Monk and serves the same purpose. The guard may use the high post as a screen, or simply make a hard cut. The important teaching point is that this cut will start to put the defense under pressure by forcing them into scramble. The diagrams and explanations are easy to follow and are brief.

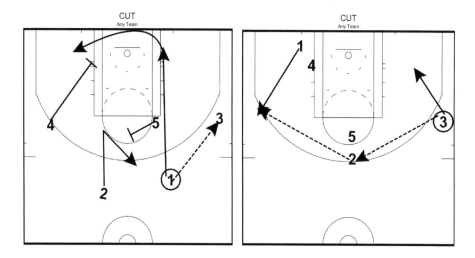

The initial pass is made from the guard (1) to the wing (3) and 1 cuts hard to basket. He may use 5 as a screener or he may not, but the idea is to go through quickly. He continues to move through as drawn, and hesitates there. 5 moves up high and screens for 2 who sets his man up and breaks to get the pass. Upon receiving the pass from 3, he quickly takes two dribbles to the weak side and makes the pass to 1 who has come off of 4's screen. It is important that the ball moves quickly to the weak side. The timing on this reversal is important. See coaching point #2 for an explanation.

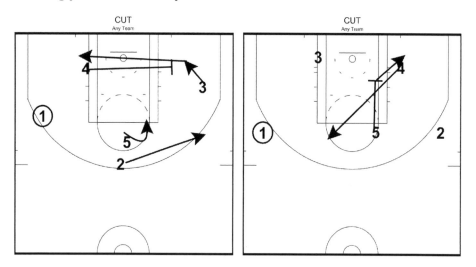

As soon as 1 cuts off of 4 to receive the pass from 2, 4 breaks to the opposite lane line to screen for 3 who walks his man into the screen and cuts baseline to the ball-side post-up. 5 positions him for screening any opponent coming up the middle of the lane. Also, 2 moves away from the ball to the weak side wing. As soon as 3 cuts, 4 quickly cuts to the elbow on ball-side.

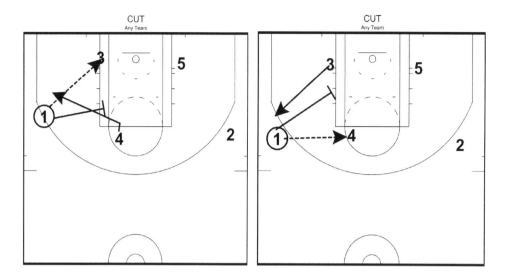

The 1 man may pass to either 3 in the post-up or 4 breaking to the elbow. If he passes to 3 in the post-up, he is a screener for 4—this is a split and all stunts may be used. If he passes to 4 at the elbow, he uses a screen down on 3. Usually either pass will result in a good shot, but the screening situations provide movement and additional scoring opportunities.

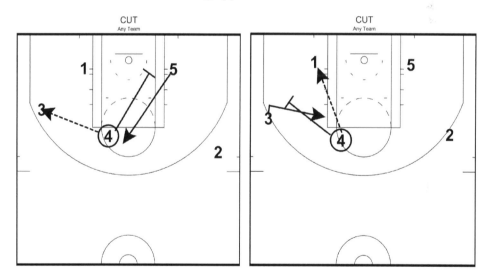

If 4 passes to 3 cutting off of 1's screen down, he (4) in turn screens down on weak side post man who cuts to the elbow. If 4 passes to 1 in the post-up position, he sets a screen for 3 which is a split. On any of the screen downs all stunts can be used.

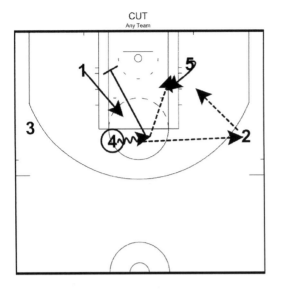

This is a powerful scoring situation. 4 at the elbow with the ball may find his best option after the screen down by 1 is to look weak side. When he looks, 5 should step in aggressively and if he gets his man behind him 4 can dump a pass into him even if he must take a few dribbles to get the right angle. If 5's defensive man gets in position to stop the step in, 4 passes to 2 who now has a great angle to get the ball into 5.

COACHING POINTS FOR CUT

1) On the initial pass to start the offense, the cutting guard (1) should cut hard and move to the weak side block if he doesn't receive a pass from the wing. He should delay slightly to let the screen down get in position, and then makes a quick cut to the wing. This delay is important for the correct timing of the play.

2) The cutting guard (1) should delay and wait for the guard at the top to receive the pass and then cut immediately, even if screen is not set. It is important that this maneuver doesn't slow the reverse pass down.

3) It is important that the ball is reversed on this play, so teach the weak side guard (2) and the high post to work together to free the guard for a pass.

4) When the guard gets the ball at the top he should reverse the ball as quickly as he can. A two step dribble helps to get a better angle for the pass to the cutter. Usually that pass is not difficult, but if the cutter is overplayed, he

uses the Monk rule and makes a back cut. When this happens and is not successful the play is broken and the team should move into the Monk offense.

5) The wing man, who frees up the cutting guard with a delay screen, goes across the lane quickly to set a screen for the opposite wing man (3) who *walks* his man down until the screen is set and then makes a hard baseline cut. We discourage cutting over the top of the screen because we are trying to drag the defensive man on 4 off to help on the cutter. If the defensive player on 4 steps to help on the cutter, 4 will get an easy shot at the elbow. If the defensive player doesn't help, 3 will get a lay-up.

6) That baseline cutter should not float out if he does not receive a pass, but work to get a good post up position which sets him up for a down screen.

7) After 5 helps the top guard he turns toward the baseline screen and starts moving down the lane watching the screening situation. As soon as 3 cuts, 5 attempts to screen any opponent. This does not need to be a head hunter screen, just delay the defensive man.

8) When 3 cuts, 4 immediately makes his cut to the ball side elbow. He should never delay this. This is a "screen the screener" play and we get a significant amount of open shots for this player at the elbow.

9) Don't worry about switches on this play. Just run it normally and the defense will make mistakes. The players will want to make adjustments, but we found that staying with the play created enough problems for the defense. This part of the play produced very good shots for either the baseline cutter, or the cut to the elbow.

10) The players are allowed the freedom to use their stunts on all screening situations and this may cause the play to breakdown. If this happens the team should move into Monk without delay.

Cut is a continuity offense that is not difficult to learn. The coaching points, though, are very important and should be attended to. The diagrams show all of the continuity, but in a game it very seldom gets that far. However, to properly prepare your team it is best to practice the team through the entire continuity. There are options in which the players are encouraged to use any of their stunts. These have already been given in Monk. Teaching Monk first enhances this offense and that is why we feel they are a good compliment.

CUT 2

The stunts are the essence of this play and the mechanics of these stunts are the same as the screen down stunts in Monk and Cut, but are enhanced by the use of two screen downs at the same time. This requires more team work and awareness of the other player's movements. Some of these stunts are in the diagrams but there are others that can be improvised at the time.

It isn't the number of stunts but the execution of them that brings exceptional results. There is a lot of the creativeness and improvisation of the Monk offense in this play. In addition to the screen down stunts, there is the possibility for a pass to the screeners, who make the same moves as in screen downs. The simplicity of the play and the numerous scoring situations are what makes it effective.

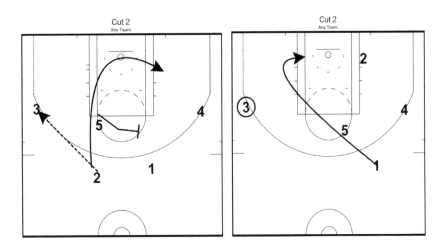

The initial cut by 2 and the movement of the high post (5) are the same as in Cut. In Cut 2 the weak side guard (1) sets his man up as in Cut, but makes a cut to the basket off of the screen.

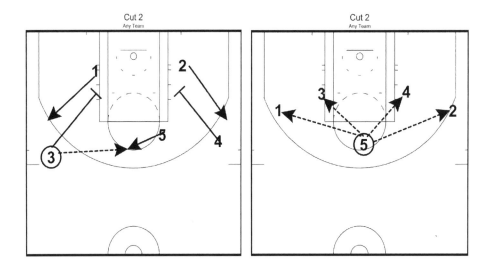

If the pass is not made to either cutter (1 or 2), the pass is made to the high-post man who comes back to receive it. Both the passer and the weak side wing man go down to set screens at the lane line. 5 now has 4 passing options as shown in diagram on right.

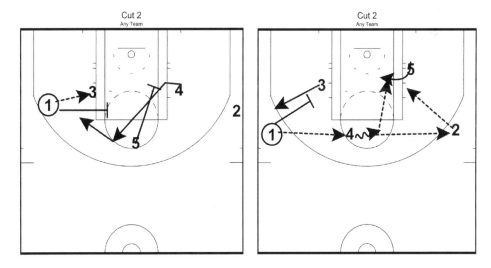

If the pass is made to the cutter at the wing, the high post screens down on the weak side post up man. If the wing man with the ball passes to the post-up he runs a split with the player at the top — in this case (4). If the wing with the ball chooses he may pass to the player at the top and run a screen down with the post player, or 4 may use the maneuver as shown in the Diagram to the right. This move is the same as in Cut.

The cuts shown are traditional cuts and many times are enough, but using the stunts on the initial screen downs provide the opportunity for the unpredictability and improvisation that is the essence of Cut 2. Some of the possibilities are shown below:

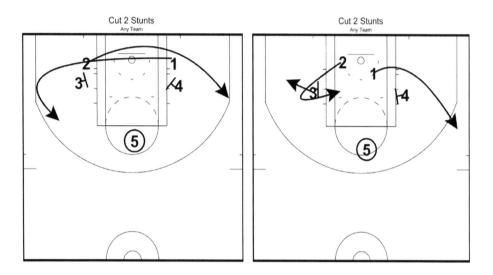

On the left is the most basic stunt, simply crossing before making cuts. Diagram on the right shows a traditional cut on one side and a curl on the other side.

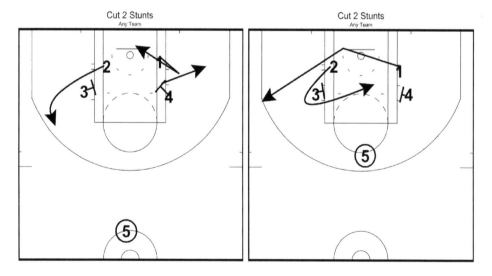

On the left is a traditional cut on one side and a back-cut on the other side. On the right is a curl followed by a traditional cut.

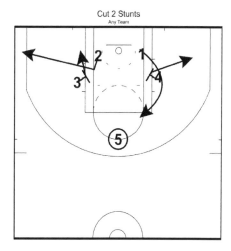
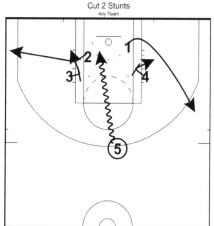

The left diagram shows a flare on one side and a baby curl on the other side. The right diagram shows a flare and a traditional cut, and a drive by the top man with the ball. It is surprising how open this drive is at times.

CUT 2 COACHING POINTS

1) On the initial guard cuts, the second cutter should be alert to occasionally go behind the screen. The wing with the ball should always take a look at both the first and second cutters for a possible pass.

2) The 5 man should turn and face the basket as soon as he gets the ball. He should look wide, so he can see both screening situations. Instruct him to be aware of a direct pass to the screeners as this is open many times.

3) Instruct the cutters not to hurry their cuts, but execute the best cut. They need to be aware of what the other cutter is doing. The cutters can and should talk on this play.

4) Encourage crossing the cutters before the stunts, but it isn't mandatory.

5) The cutters (guards) need a lot of repetition on the stunts shown in the diagrams.

Normally Cut 2 will be called, but there is another and very effective method of getting into it. We not only allow this option, we encourage it as it makes both Cut and Cut 2 more effective. If Cut is called but the weak side guard is overplayed on the screen by 5, he may back cut to the basket. This cut turns the play from Cut into Cut 2 and the other players adjust immediately. This may appear to be difficult but the players catch on to it quite quickly. Because it is spontaneous it is very difficult for the defense. This can be incorporated as soon as both Cut and Cut 2 are well learned. It is simple but it opens a number of scoring options.

AUTOMATIC

This is an excellent play that provides unpredictability and the opportunity for a three point shot. The name comes from the fact that it is run anytime the ball is thrown to the High Post player, regardless of what play has been called. It can be used anytime there is difficulty getting the ball into the wing. The players do not need to know it is coming, but they must be able to react quickly when the pass to the high post is made.

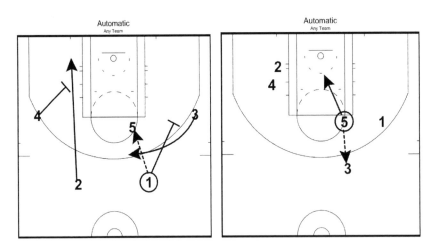

Automatic is initiated on any pass from guard to the high post regardless of what play has been called. The passing guard (1) moves quickly to set a screen for the wing player on the same side. The weak side guard (2) makes a hard cut to the lane line on his side, and the wing man on that side is ready to make a screen down. If the defensive player on the strong side is forced to go behind the screen by the guard, it will force him to go behind the high post man which opens up a three point attempt for the wing man. After the hand off, the high-post cuts to the basket taking his man out of the play.

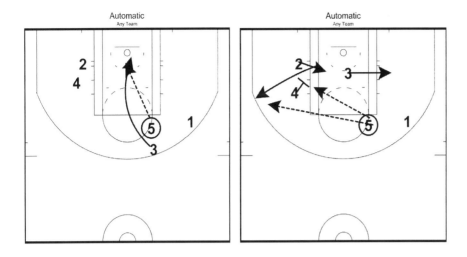

The technique of the 5 man is discussed later but if he can't pass to 3 and 3 continues down the lane as shown he should look for the pass over the shoulder of the cutter, as many times the defensive man trails which provides a lay-up. If that pass is not available, the high-post man with the ball turns and looks at the weak-side. This look triggers the screen down by 4 on 2.

The stunts developed by the screen of the guard on the wing player are the same as the stunts in a post-up split. It is difficult for the defense because it is in a different floor position. The high position of the wing and the high-post creates openness for cuts to the basket which must be respected by the defense or a lay-up will ensue.

Automatic requires special training for the high post player and these instructions are described in the coaching points.

The coach and players should not overlook the overhead pass in the third frame and the weak side play that is in the next frame. The threat of the overhead pass tends to freeze the defensive players on the weak side and makes the weak side screen down very effective.

AUTOMATIC STUNTS

The stunts diagramed below are the same basic stunts that are used in low-post splits. The success of this play requires good use of these stunts.

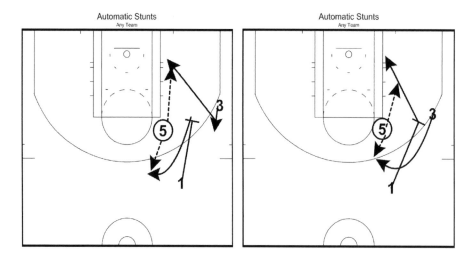

On the left is a simple back-cut by the wing man if his man tries to get over the top of the screen. If 3 uses the back-cut option the screener becomes the player going over the top of the high-post. The diagram on the right is a roll by the screener to the basket and 3 goes over the top as he would normally. If 1 does not get the pass he should work himself back to the wing position

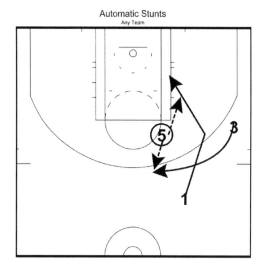

This diagram is not a roll by the screener; instead it shows the screener slipping the screen and the wing man going over the top.

COACHING POINTS FOR AUTOMATIC

1) As soon as the pass is made to the high post both guards take the routes diagramed. The wing man sets his man up for the guard's screen. He

should attempt to get his defensive man to go behind this screen. This will force his defensive man to go behind 5, and open a shot at the top. The screener and the cutter have many options as shown in the diagrams of the stunts.

2) When 5 receives the pass he does not turn but stays flat with a strong grip on the ball. He needs to see the screen situation on the entry side out of the corner of his eye as this is where the basket cuts will develop.

3) 5's rule is if the cutter comes over the top he should pass to him if there is no defensive player between him and the cutter. If this pass is made, he makes a hard cut to the basket. If the defensive player gets between him and the cutter he pivots on his inside foot and follows the cutter around. This acts as a slight screen and positions him to make the overhead pass to the cutter going down the middle of the lane.

4) When the 5 man turns to look at the weak side 4 moves to set the screen down and 2 can make any screen down cut.

5) 5 is taught the various passes he can use. He must be alert to see cutters if they use one of the stunts. If either 1 or 3 (as shown in initial diagram) cut to the basket and he gets them the ball it is usually a lay-up.

6) This is a wonderful play to get a three point shot if you have wing players that can make that shot. If they are taught how to run the play they will get a lot of 3 point opportunities. Effectively using all the stunts of this screening situation allows the 3 point shot to open.

ADDITIONAL THOUGHTS ON THE SET OFFENSE

Out of Bounds plays, Go To plays, Need plays, and End of Quarter plays have not been included; each coach should determine these. There is one suggestion on Out of Bounds plays. Use Monk instead of a set play. Our research is consistent that out of bounds plays are not effective. The defense is set on these plays and it is extremely difficult to get good shots. The unpredictability of the Monk offense puts pressure on a set defense, as it forces them into scramble.

I would like to comment about set plays in general. I have some questions and some irritations with the common repertoire of plays. I have studied plays in the NBA and college for some years, and I am at a loss to understand what I see. The following paragraphs are my personal thoughts and they may be contrary to what others think.

The tendency of coaches is to have a lot of plays. Some teams have 40 or 50 of them. Any scouting report will show that each play is run only a few times and they are not very effective. It is very difficult for players to learn nuances of these plays. Plays require intricate timing, coordination, and experience. Set plays are run against a set defense and that requires more precise execution. Players need repetitions in practice and in games to become comfortable with the details of a play. From this repetition they learn the refinements of the play, and how they can best execute it. Jumping from one play to another does not allow this and it results in poor execution.

Earlier chapters show how ineffective plays are, but it is not the plays; it is the lackluster execution and this can be due to unfamiliarity. A good example of the advantages in learning a play thoroughly is the Triangle. It is a very simple offense and the coach never changes it. Yet it has won 11 NBA championships because the players execute it to perfection. They have the knowledge of the offense to do this. That knowledge comes from repeated practice and play. They don't try different things; they perfect what they are doing.

There is one other point I would like to leave you with. It is physical play. This type of defense can be very disruptive to a team offense. It results, many times, in bad shots and turnovers. Physical play is easy to use against a stand around offense like two man plays, such as middle screen and roll. This puts the onus on players to make tough shots. Movement changes this. It is difficult to be physical when you are chasing your man.***

CHAPTER SEVENTEEN

ZONE OFFENSE

Playing a different type of game.

If you have followed and taught the offensive information in this book you are 90 percent ready for the zone defense. The Monk system has a simple strategy for playing against zone defenses. It is to use the Monk offense exclusively. There are some adjustments, but they are simple and easy to learn.

There are some attributes of the zone defense that are different from man-to-man and require some changes in the offensive attack. The ball position dictates the movement of the zone—called shifts. Offensive players are only noticed if they are in a player's zone and once the offensive player leaves a zone, the defensive player in that zone releases him—he does not follow him. This shifting and releasing creates gaps in the zone.

Gaps are brief holes in the zone that can be penetrated with a pass, a cut, or a dribble. They can appear any place in the defense. They are created by movement of the ball and movement of the players. These gaps are vulnerable because offensive players can move into them as no one in the zone defense is responsible for them. There are also other attributes of the zone.

The man with the ball is not played the same as in a man-to-man defense. The player with the ball is defended by the player in that zone and is defended softer in a zone defense. If the man with the ball drives, the player in that zone releases him to the player in the next zone. Penetration of the ball by drives is very harmful to the zone defense because there can be confusion as to who is responsible for him.

The zone is a weak rebounding defense, because no one has responsibility for a man. If the offense is aggressive in going to the ball they will get many second shot opportunities and these are usually a high percentage shot.

The zone defense takes the position that they will clog up the middle—hoping to stop drives-- at the expense of giving up the outside shot. Thus many offenses are lured into trying to beat the zone with outside shooting which is what the zone wants.

An important consideration with the zone defense is its inability to set up quickly to stop transition after a defensive rebound or steal. Any quick exchange of ball possession, such as defensive rebounds and steals, give it problems.

The zone has its drawbacks as a defense, but it can be troublesome. It cuts down on lay-ups, especially if the offense does not aggressively rebound. Even more troublesome, it tends to change the rhythm of the game. It slows the game down which creates problems for the offense, breaking up its momentum. Furthermore, very few coaches have an effective zone offense because they don't like to practice against a zone so preparation is limited, and an offense can be ineffective.

MONK OFFENSE VERSUS THE ZONE

The Monk offense—with very little adjustment—has the elements that are effective against the zone defense. First, it has exceptional player and ball movement which gives the shifting of the zone great problems. Second, it has the ability to attack quickly in transition before the zone can get set. Both of these attributes are part of the Monk offense and will not require new learning. If the team is properly coached, the Monk offense will have little trouble with a zone.

It does require a few simple adjustments that we will discuss. Use of the screen is limited and the emphasis is on driving and cutting into the gaps of the zone. Of course, this is where the zone is vulnerable. Also, offensive rebounding is not only emphasized but demanded.

In the half-court, the Monk offense is started the same way as it starts against a man-to-man defense; two guards, two wings, and a high-post. The first pass is to the wing and the passer makes the same cut as in the man-to-man offense. This initial cut is very important. It forces the zone defense to make some difficult shifts. The same Monk offense rules are used but our terminology is slightly different. In the zone offense we *drive into gaps, and cut into holes.* The teaching and learning procedure is minimized because the Monk offense requires nothing new.

GAPS: DRIVES, CUTS, AND PASSES

It is important to understand the philosophy of gaps. It will take a little time and patience for the inexperienced coach and player to recognize these gaps because they appear quickly and unpredictably. I will attempt to show them with diagrams, but they are only learned with extensive scrimmage and game experience. There are no shortcuts.

They occur because of the nature of the zone defense; that is, players don't guard a man—instead, they defend a prescribed area. They adjust their positions within that area depending on where the ball is. When they make that adjustment it is termed "shifts". These shifts create gaps or holes. Offensive players need to have the freedom to make cuts and drives into them when they occur. The Monk offense gives them that because it trains them to use this freedom.

These gaps occur if the offense moves players and ball. Sometimes it will take time to find them, and then to cut or drive into them. There are no drills to teach this—other than those used in the Monk offense. Players need to practice 5 versus 5 to learn the movement, cuts, drives, and passes used in playing against a zone. Don't wait until an opponent uses a zone defense; be prepared for it. The controlled scrimmage, 5 versus 5 explained in the Monk offense training chapters, is excellent for this.

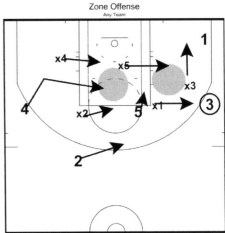

The diagrams above show two possible situations that these gaps may occur. The gaps are shown as shaded areas (blue). When 1 passes and cuts through the zone, and x3 takes the ball at the wing it opens up two gaps; one at the middle of the lane, and the other in the corner (Frame to left). If x1 takes the ball at the wing, it opens gaps shown; one on the lane, and another in the middle of the lane. The frame on the right shows possible cuts into these gaps.

The Frame to the left shows 1 cutting to the weak side and this freezes x5 who must take him temporarily. The gaps are shown. In the frame to the right, wing player 1 throws a cross court pass and this provides 3 gaps.

In the flow of the game there will be many possibilities for gaps. In time, players will learn to recognize the gaps and the holes so they can quickly react to these opportunities either with a cut or a drive.

PATIENCE

As mentioned earlier, the zone defense tends to slow the offensive attack down. This is not because the offense slows down, but because it takes more time to find the openings. In a half-court situation, the players must be patient, but aggressive. It is a test of their will to sustain aggressive cuts, drives, and movement for an extended time. Once they have learned this, the result will be easy shots.

SHOT SELECTION

As the zone defense protects the middle well, there will be opportunities for outside shots. Teams do not win many games depending on outside shooting. The offense must work to break the zone down and get inside shots—especially lay-ups. This will happen with good movement and patience. Many teams take the first open outside shot that they get, rather than wait a few more passes for a higher percentage inside shot. They play into the zone's strength when they do this.

REBOUNDING

A zone defense has trouble with rebounding. Many of the best shots are available from offensive rebounding. In a conference I coached in, there was a good coach that utilized this aspect for great success. His unique strategy against a zone was to have his players in a position to rebound, and encouraged shooting so that his team could rebound missed shots. In the Monk offense we use both methods; to move, cut, drive, and pass for shots, and to put 4 men on the offensive boards when a shot is taken. This can result in high percentage shots.

TRANSITION

The zone has trouble getting set when a team fast breaks. They may be able to control the first part of the fast break, but they will not be set in their zone positions for Monk. This period of time when the fast break ends but an aggressive offense follows is very difficult for the zone. At this time they are very vulnerable to cuts and drives. The Monk offense is trained for this situation—to fast break to Monk. If it is well done, and sustained, it can be a game changer.

****

At most levels the zone defense only provides problems for teams if they are not prepared. Unfortunately, many teams do not prepare at all. I find it interesting that so little zone is played in the NBA, because most NBA teams do not know how to play against it. The Monk Offense has filled the bill very well over the years. Not only does it work well against a zone defense, but it requires less preparation time as most of the skills are learned in the day to day use of the offense.

CHAPTER EIGHTEEN

FAST BREAK AND MONK

Self-Trust is the essence of heroism

Ralph Waldo Emerson
Heroism

The Fast Break is planned but unstructured. It is not a space, but it creates a space. It takes only 4 to 5 seconds to perform, and though coaches try to structure it--in games it is freelance. The fast break is followed by transition—a component of the third element. In the Monk system, the fast break is followed automatically with Monk which is our approach to transition. The fast break is the first phase and takes place with controlled speed. If it fails to produce an appropriate shot, it flows smoothly into Monk without allowing the defense to get set. This combination of fast break and Monk is a relentless attack and a powerful offensive weapon. Because it is uncertain where the ball will be, where the players will be, and where the defense will be, there is no practical way an organized approach can be reliable.

When I was an assistant coach with the Orlando Magic, Paul Westhead was also an assistant and in charge of the fast break. Paul was a passionate and committed proponent of the fast break and in his mind it was all you needed to win. He developed a way to structure the fast break, and he artfully designed it to cover all situations—he even structured a fast break after made baskets. He was a wonderful teacher of his system and I admired his organization.

Still, in looking at films, his structure broke down in games, even after made baskets. Certainly, we scored points off of the fast break and he made the Magic a fast break team. However, realistically most of the points came in transition which was not structured. Afterwards, as I reflected on Paul and his fast break I came to the conclusion that he needed to be the head coach in order to have his system succeed and then succeed it would.

For the rest of us, the fast break results in a shot only 36 percent of the time; it does not get a shot 64 percent of the time. But, the shots obtained in this phase are normally very high percentage shots. The consistent quick attack of the fast break is important because it is necessary to set up the flow into Monk. This combined attack puts terrific pressure on the defense, with the Monk portion providing most of the shots and most of the points. To evaluate the effectiveness of this attack, fast break and transition should be analyzed as a unit. For the sake of clarity, it is not done that way in this book; but as a coach I consider them as a unit.

In the Monk system, we only fast break after defensive rebounds or steals and players do not run to the three point line; we run for lay ups. It is easy in the fast break to get a three point shot, but it should be taken only by a competent shooter who is uncontested. Monk, in transition, is a higher producer of points than questionable three point shots taken in the fast break phase. Constantly remind your players of this.

The key to a successful fast break attack is the outlet pass. Hours of charting films has proven that the outlet pass must be made between the top of the three point line and the time line. The outlet player receiving the pass must get to this area though he can be in the middle or on the side. This is shown in the diagrams that follow.

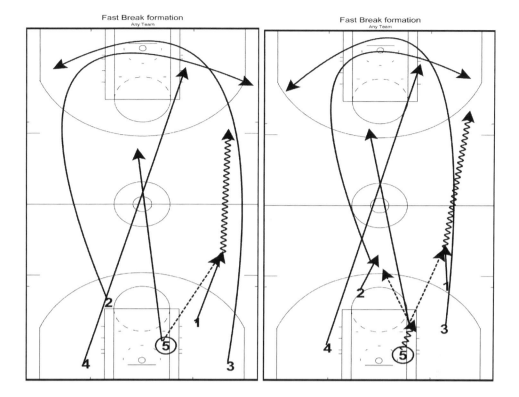

Fast Break formation
Any Team

Fast Break formation
Any Team

These diagrams show the ideal formation that is desired. It is seldom run like this in game conditions. The most important aspect is the outlet pass and the position of the receiver or outlet man. Once the ball is outlet the rest of the team sprints to the basket. They attempt to cross at the basket out to the wings; the other players fill the post-up and the top of the three point circle as shown.

We emphasize the crossing of the earliest players to develop an opportunity for a lay-up. We encourage the players to cross even if there is no one to cross with. At least one player should cross as this keeps the defense unsettled for the attack with Monk. Players must learn to sprint—not jog—on the break without regard to certain lanes; just get there as fast as you can under control. Monk is started immediately if the fast break fails to produce a shot, regardless of where the players are; the player with the ball simply passes to a wing and cuts through to initiate the Monk offense; he may also dribble to the wing position to start it.

FAST BREAK RULES

1) The defensive rebounder must be in a position to make the longer outlet pass right away. If obstructed, he uses a power dribble to clear himself for the pass to the outlet man.

2) The outlet receiver must quickly get to the outlet position desired. This is a skill that can be learned. It is possible to have two players to outlet to; one should be in the middle and one on the side that the ball is rebounded.

3) All players away from the ball sprint to the opposite basket. This is not a jog, it is controlled speed.

4) The first players down the floor cross as shown in the diagram. They cross even if there is no one to cross with.

5) The next player, after the crossing players, should go to the post up position.

6) The last player fills—this may be to the top or to a wing. There will be times when Monk is started by the time this player gets to the half-court; he should adjust accordingly and become a part of the Monk attack.

If, in the fast break, a high percentage shot is available, it should be taken. However, it has to be the right shot, because flowing into Monk will provide good shots and proficiency in scoring. The players must be trained to understand this shot selection. Remember that the team will have about 18 seconds to run Monk for a good shot, so it is not necessary to hurry.

We use two drills to develop our fast break and Monk attack. The initial drill is a 5 man drill that incorporates the total attack plan. The only breakdown drill is a two man fast break drill. The 2 man fast break drill and the 5 man drill are shown next.

TWO MAN FAST BREAK DRILL

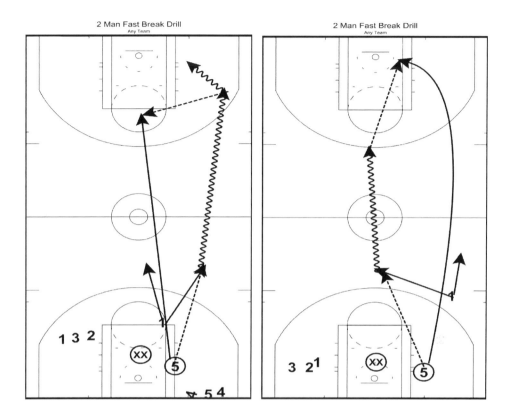

Players should be in groups of two; a ball handler and a rebounder. Each group should have a ball. The outlet man is at the free throw line, and the rebounder is at the basket. As a group of two takes these positions, they hand their ball to the coach, and the coach throws the ball on to the backboard, making it easy for the rebounder to obtain the ball. Once the rebounder controls the ball, the outlet player breaks to an outlet position and the rebounder outlets quickly. The ball handler takes a middle lane or a side lane, and the rebounder takes the other lane closest to him. The ball handler keeps the ball and drives it to the scoring end. He then delivers a pass to the sprinting rebounder for either a lay-up or a short jump shot. The ball handler may also take either one of those shots. Do not let the outlet man break early. Each group of two will stay at the scoring end until all groups have finished. Then the coach at that end starts the same drill on the other side.

This drill teaches the coordination between rebounder and outlet receiver. It also creates the shots that will be taken on the break: Jump shot at FT Line or Wing, layup from the wing and layup by the dribbler. We ask either player filling the middle lane to stop at the free throw line unless he is confident a cut to the basket is open for a layup. Players need to practice the free throw line jump shot.

71

FIVE MAN FAST BREAK DRILL

This drill combines all aspects of the fast break and Monk. The coach misses a shot attempt and on possession of the ball, the team initiates and runs a fast break. If no shot is taken in the fast break phase, they move seamlessly into Monk offense. The coach may have to instruct them to pass up a shot on the fast break and move into Monk so they get comfortable with doing that. The coach may also throw the ball on the floor to simulate a steal. After some skill is obtained we begin to change the player's positions on defense so that they understand the technique of organizing the fast break from any position. The mechanics of doing this will be explained in a rebounding drill presented in the defensive chapters.

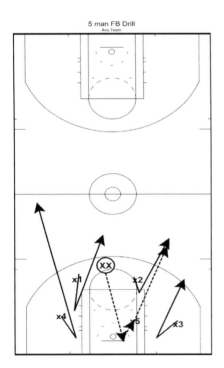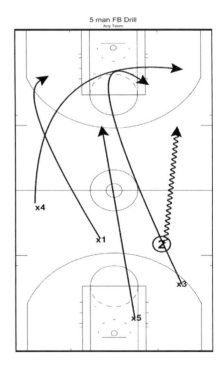

All five players face the coach in a defensive position. The coach may move players by moving the ball. The coach shoots to miss and team rebounding rules apply. All five players are rebounders. Do not let the rebounders start running before the rebound is secured. Once the ball is secured by any player, the rest follow the fast break rules. They break to the other end and can get a shot off of the break, or they can move into Monk. There should be another group of five ready to go, and the first group stays at the far end.

I am convinced that these two drills are all you need to develop a very effective fast break and Monk combination. These two drills along with experience built in the half-court, full-court drill (explained in the Monk offense section) as well as periodic scrimmaging provide all the skill work necessary. If your defense is good you can expect to get between 35 and 40 opportunities to fast break and about 26 to 28 of these will end in Monk. Many teams do not use all the opportunities to break, and call a play instead. Teams that do this lose out on the opportunity to play against a defense that is not set. In essence, they are trading a positive possession (POP) for a negative possession (NOP). When the decision is made to stop the break and run a play, a team is giving up an opportunity that usually scores .91 points per possession for a possession that scores .58 points. Assuming that there are 36 opportunities in a game and the team does this each time, they would score 12 points less on those possessions. This is giving up a lot of points.

This explanation may seem brief and simple, but the fast break is brief and simple. There is still a lot of coaching to do, but the nature of the fast break, like improvisation, requires simplicity. Players need this simplicity to free themselves for spontaneous reactions.

Remember that the fast break emanates from a successful defense that produces ample defensive rebounds and steals. Defense is the key, and will be explained next.

CHAPTER NINETEEN

DEFENSE

Why Defend?
Because it wins.

I can remember the very evening that my defensive philosophy was established. I was just starting my first collegiate coaching position at a Division III school—Winona State University. For some time, my assistant and I had been meeting each evening in a classroom working out plans for the upcoming season. We had been working on defense, and had put up on the board innumerable situations that we felt we had to defend. Each situation created a challenge for us and our solutions were many times confusing because our technique for one situation contradicted a technique prescribed for another. I was frustrated in having to remember all these different techniques. Eventually, I just stopped, and there was a prolonged period of silence while we stared at the blackboard.

Finally it came to me, and I said out loud, "why can't we have a simple system that will apply to all situations?" We began to strive for that. It started with a single concept; we wanted five defensive players between the man with the ball and the basket. That became "The Ball Line Defense". That very evening we did not leave until we had built 10 very simple rules, rules that have stayed with me everywhere I have coached. Coaches that have worked with me and players that have played for me use the same rules.

Fast forward some forty years. I was working in my office while an assistant with the Cleveland Cavaliers, when the phone rang. When I picked it up the voice introduced himself as a writer covering the finals of the NCAA tournament in which Kentucky was playing. He wanted to interview me because in a press conference the Kentucky coach, Tubby Smith, had given me credit for their highly regarded defense. He was referring to the Ball Line Defense. I did not know Tubby Smith, but I learned later that he had been an assistant to one of my former assistants, J.D. Barnett and J.D. was using the defense we had used while he was with me.

The story gets stranger. Tubby Smith moved to the University of Minnesota and I was curious to see if he still used the defense. So I called him. He said he was using the ball line defense and had used it at every college he had coached. I asked him to send me the rules as I felt he must have made changes over the years. When I received them I had the strangest feeling—they were the exact same rules that we had developed on that late night session, in a bare classroom at Winona State University. It was surreal to see those same rules, word for word, that we had developed so many years ago. And they are the same rules I will provide in the next chapter.

It has been pointed out, many times, that in scramble the defense is in trouble. Scramble is closely associated with the spaces, so the defense will be in that position a significant portion of the game. Very few, if any, teams can sustain success without a respectable defense. Knowing that so much of the game is played in the spaces, under the duress of scramble, it is essential to have a defense that can handle the unpredictability that occurs in these spaces.

The dilemma is how does a team play effective defense when they have no idea what the offense will do? The position that I take, and is the foundation of this defense, is to strip away the strategies and boil it down to the raw essence, which is individual effort. Granted, there has to be some form of team organization. I believe this is best applied with the use of rules that are simple and flexible. Fixed plans, such as rotations, will not survive in the chaos of scramble. It is imperative that a team prepares for these situations; first to prevent being in scramble, and secondly to effectively play defense if scramble happens. A simple set of rules and a strong commitment to these rules is the answer.

The following pages will describe the ball line defense. To prepare the reader I will state at this time that the rules and the philosophy of this defense will differ slightly from most, if not all, defenses. But before explaining this defense, I feel it is important to provide a concept that is paramount to any defense—

namely The Three Pillars of Defense.

THE THREE PILLARS OF DEFENSE

The three pillars of defense are: contain the ball, contest shots, and rebound. That statement sounds easy. It is not easy, but it is highly effective. It is not easy to train players to excel at these three simple skill. It discourages most coaches. It is easier to rely on a strategy than to work with players and insist on their accepting the individual responsibility of perfecting the above three principles.

The readers that have come this far probably have grasped the vulnerability of scramble defense, and the large portion of a game that a team has to play in it. Please add the next statement to the depth of your knowledge. *The defense, by giving help, puts itself in scramble.* If you don't have to give help, you do not need to rotate and rotating is scramble because the defense is no longer set; rotating is a trap you set for yourself.

The first pillar of defense is the containment of the ball by one player without requiring help. We are speaking, when we use the word containment, of keeping the man with the ball from penetrating the defense with a dribble. This puts the burden squarely on the person guarding the ball. This is quite different from popular thinking which teaches otherwise. They teach schemes to give help, such as rotations, double-teams and other helping strategies and these all create scramble. These schemes may be successful in stopping a known offensive situation such as plays, but they crash in the unpredictability of scramble-- which they created.

Players, and unfortunately coaches, contend that a defensive player cannot control, by himself, a good offensive player. That is poppycock. They can't because they do not train to do it. *If they spend as much time learning to defend penetration, as the offensive player spends learning how to penetrate, they will be effective.*

The truth is that coaches spend their time on rotations and schemes with hardly any time on man on man containment. It is self destructive, and it is a weak psychology to base a player's defense on help. It gives the player a crutch, destroys motivation to defend, and provides a built in excuse.

It is necessary to qualify our thoughts on playing defense this way. A team defense may give help in a hidden manner without forcing themselves into scramble. This is accomplished by the ball line defensive positions away from the ball. To the offensive player with the ball, it looks difficult to penetrate. The ball line defense, then, stops penetration with position rather than help. This is discussed in the next chapter.

The Second Pillar is contesting shots. There should be little argument on this because the difference in shooting success between a contested shot and an uncontested shot is huge. In the study outlined in Chapter Three, it was demonstrated that a contested shot had a field goal percentage of 36 percent, while an uncontested shot was 68 percent. It is obvious that contesting shots is essential to good defense.

Yet I would venture a guess there are few, if any, coaches in the NBA that work on contesting shots; by that I mean actually practicing the skill, not just lip service. I hope I am wrong. In college, I believe you would find coaches that do work on it but probably not many.

The Third Pillar is defensive rebounding. A defensive rebound has double power. First it ends the offensive team's possession in which they did not score. Secondly, it gives the defensive team an opportunity to fast break into transition— a positive possession (POP). Chapter three shows that defensive rebounds have, along with steals, a direct impact on winning.

I am very emphatic that a team strong in these three pillars will be a good defensive team regardless of the strategy used. Whatever defensive strategy is used, it eventually breaks down if a team cannot effectively apply these three skills. It is imperative that the coach teaches, motivates, and insists on a responsible attitude of the players in their defense. It will win games.

CHAPTER TWENTY

BALL LINE DEFENSE

It is easy in the world to live after the worlds opinion, it is easy in solitude to live after our own, but the great man is he who in the midst of the crowd keeps with perfect sweetness the independence of solitude.

Self-Reliance
Ralph Waldo Emerson

OVERVIEW

The Ball Line defense is a rule defense. Instead of a defense designed to stop specific offensive situations, such as plays, it is guided by simple and easy to understand rules which can be applied in any situation. It is not burdensome as it does not have numerous situations to remember and execute. There are only 10 basic rules and a few ancillary rules for specific situations, which are simple and brief.

The entire Monk system is based on the knowledge that much of each game is played when there is no structure. This creates an unpredictable offensive attack, and a defense designed for structured plays has difficulty coping with this. A structured defense has a specific way to handle each of a multitude of offensive strategies. There are hundreds of plays that have sophisticated procedures within them. To remember and execute in these situations is difficult, and leads to confusion because it is difficult to give players enough preparation to handle each one.

The bottom line is that for a defense to be good, it must be able to defend unpredictable play in the spaces. In the 2010 NBA finals between Boston and Los Angeles, Boston was well prepared for the Lakers' triangle offense. It was a close seven game series with games separated by just a few points. The Lakers won primarily because Boston could not defend in the spaces. The Lakers were well prepared offensively to play in these situations because they had been trained with their movement type of offense. Boston defended the triangle well, but when it failed (breakdown), and the players improvised, their defense could not cope. This was the difference in the series and gave Los Angles the championship.

The Ball Line defense is not difficult to learn but the coach plays a major role in its effectiveness. It must be well taught and players must be given ample opportunity to gain experience in its use. This can be accomplished by providing the right drills, scrimmage play, game play, and intelligent instruction. The material for doing this is included in the next few chapters. The place to start is with the rules.

BALL LINE DEFENSE RULES

BASIC RULES

1) Always retreat quickly to the ball line.
2) Contest all shots
3) See ball and man
4) Overplay penetrating passes i.e. passes that move the ball closer to the basket.
5) Allow non-penetrating passes.
6) Play as close to the ball as possible but must be able to deflect or intercept a pass to own man.
7) Front any player in the paint.
8) Trap all mismatches in the post up.
9) Go for blocked shot over trying for the charge.
10) Help only when needed, such as a layup threat.

POST PLAY DEFENSE

1) Force post player off the block with overplay or contact.
2) Front any player in the paint area.

DEFENDING THE DRIVE

1) Force drive to middle where defensive players are positioned.
2) Control drive by an imaginary 8' box from the basket without fouling
3) Influence the driver to take a runner rather than a pull up jump shot.

SCREEN AT THE BALL DEFENSE

1) Containing the drive is the highest priority.
2) Screener's man loosens up.
3) Man on ball goes under screen to stop drive.
4) Switch if necessary. On a switch, front the roll man and control the man with ball.

SCREEN AWAY FROM THE BALL

1) Go ball side of screen except on anticipated flare cut.

2) Screener's man loosens but with a quick recovery to his man.

3) Switch if necessary, but only if threatened.

FULL COURT DEFENSE

1) ¾ Court man pressure after dead ball possessions.

2) Use trap as directed.

3) Use Run and Jump as directed.

The rules are written in poor English grammar and structure. This is done to make each rule as brief as possible. This is important to help in remembering and reacting to instruction. The rules are simple, the words are simple.

EXPLANATION OF BALL LINE RULES

To be blind is bad, but worse it is to have eyes and not to see.

Helen Keller

The rules are stated very simply and with few words. This is no problem when it is being taught on the floor, but it may be a little confusing to the reader, so I am providing a more detailed explanation at this time. In the teaching chapters that follow it will be even clearer, as there will be diagrams to help with understanding.

BASIC RULES

Always retreat quickly to the Ball Line.

This is the major rule and very important in this defense. Basically, all five players need to be at the ball line or below it. For example, if the ball is at the free throw line extended there should be five defensive players between that line and the basket. This rule is applied in all situations from full court to half court. The diagram will show this clearly.

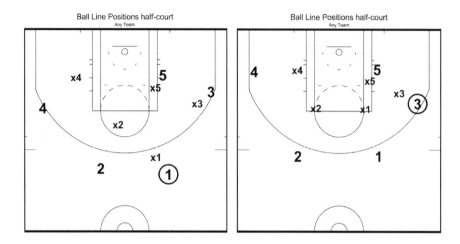

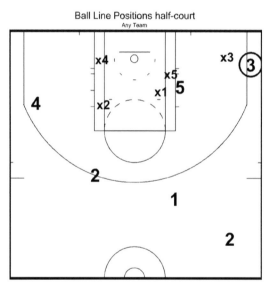

These three diagrams show the ball line positions in three half-court situations. It should be apparent how this position can discourage any attempt to drive. A full-court diagram is displayed in the drills section.

Contest all Shots

We want all shots contested regardless of whose man it is. As shown in Chapter Three there is a significant difference in the field goal percentage of contested and uncontested shots. Teams shot 68 percent on uncontested attempts, and when contested, dropped to 36 percent. One of the reasons for avoiding scramble is to have players in good position to contest all shots. The ball line positions accomplish this, and also establish good rebounding position.

See ball and Man

Vision is very necessary in good defense. The proper position is to be able to see both your man and the ball at the same time. The defensive player may have to adjust his position to do this. This is a very simple rule, but essential to good sag position.

Overplay Penetrating passes; passes that move the ball closer to the basket.

By overplay we mean to deny the offensive player the ball and force him out of the position he wants to receive it. This usually applies to the wing man, but it also applies to a post defender and to weak side players cutting to the ball side below the ball line.

Allow Non-Penetrating passes.

This applies mainly to the pass from the wing back to the top of the key as diagramed. But it also applies to any backward pass, and this is true in the full-court defense and in half-court defense. For example, a post player with the ball requires our defense to sag deeply to apply the ball line rule, which puts our players in a better position to dig, rebound, and contest. We do not attempt to stop the non-penetrating pass out to the outside players. However, we do expect the defensive man to recover to the man with the ball, at least in time to contest the shot.

Play as close to the ball as possible but be able to deflect or intercept a pass to own man.

This rule allows our weak side players to sag, but they must be able to get back to their man quickly. Each defensive player is different in their quickness. A quicker player can sag deeper than a slower player. Each player must find his own distance where he is able to deflect or intercept any pass thrown to his man.

Thus, he must change his position based on where the ball is and where his man is.

Front any player in the paint.

Fronting a post player takes us out of good defensive position. It is proper to overplay a post up player and still have good rebounding and contesting position. The player in the paint, though, is too dangerous and he must be fronted.

Trap all mismatches in the post up.

Because we allow occasional switching, when necessary, it is possible that a smaller player may be guarding a bigger player in the post-up. We trap that situation. There are other times that this can occur; the rule is for all mismatches in the post.

Try to block shots rather than trying for the charge.

In a high percentage of charge/block calls, the defense is called for a block. Seldom does the offensive player get called for a charge. Taking the charge is not nearly as effective as coach's think. The blocked shot, even if not successful, is very effective in curbing field goal percentage because it is still a good contest.

Only help in an emergency that is a lay-up threat. Be available to dig and get back to own man.

We use digging and faking but we don't go unless a threat for a lay-up is evident. It is incredible how many open shots are given to players because their defensive man is trying to help on another player. Watch any game in the NBA and see the number of times a player is open in the corner on a drive. In the NBA players make less than 40percent of their shots on a drive into the middle. This is a fact. Yet they make 68 percent of uncontested shots which they get when a player leaves to stop a 38 percent shot off the drive.

RULES FOR SPECIFIC DEFENSIVE SITUATIONS

Post Play

Force post player off the block with overplay or contact.

Ideal defensive position on a post player is a slight overplay on the side of the offensive player. Keeping a player off of the block can also be accomplished with physical play. If the defensive man can force the post player a step off the lane it neutralizes many post players.

Front if man is in the paint.

However, a player in the paint near the basket is a real threat and must be fronted. The pass to a fronted man near the basket is very difficult and fronting is worth the risk.

Playing the drive:

Force drive to middle.

If the offensive player with the ball is at the top of the key area we try to force him towards the middle but away from a direct line to the basket. On the wing we want to keep him from going baseline and force him into the help which is in the middle and should look impenetrable and discourage any attempt to drive.

Control drive by 8' box without fouling.

Most of the points scored on drives are from lay-ups, free throws, and passes by the driver to an open man. Taking away or reducing those three elements make drives ineffective. We want our players to concentrate on cutting a player off by an imaginary 8' box from the basket. Do not be physical; rather be quick to maintain a position slightly ahead of the dribbler. The defensive man's responsibility is to control the drive without fouling and allowing a lay-up. When playing like this lay-ups, free throws, and passes to uncovered players are avoided.

Force player to take short range runner.

We have found that driving into the middle and taking a runner is a very low percentage shot even for NBA players. There are very few players that can shoot this shot well. We are willing to give it up over other shots. One of these is the mid-range pull up jump shot which is effective and it must be contested.

Screen at the Ball Defense:

- Stopping the drive is the highest priority.
- Screener's man loosens up.
- Man on ball takes the best route over or under screen to stop drive.
- Switch if necessary rather than have two on the ball. On a switch, front the roll man and control the man with ball.

Of course, a team has to play against a lot of screens at the ball but they are not as effective as they seem. If you can stop penetration you take away their best play. The defensive player guarding the man with the ball should go under the screen unless it is impossible, and going over the screen is the only route. The second dangerous part of the screen at the ball is the weak side. If the defense stays contained by not overreacting to the screen portion, they will maintain good position for handling weak side play. Staying out of scramble by avoiding the use of rotations is the key. Opponents will score some, but at the end of the night, playing this way will quietly get the results desired. The screen at the ball rules are clearly explained and shown in the next chapter.

Screen without the ball involved:

- Always go on the ball side of the screen.
- Screeners man loosens, but gets right back.
- Switch if necessary but only if threatened.

Ball side means to go between the ball and the screener; this will be diagramed later in the drills portion. This requires the defensive man on the screener to loosen up so the player guarding the cutter can get through but he must get back to his man quickly. It is better to switch if the defense gets caught in a situation that allows the offense an easy shot.

Full Court Defense:

- ¾ Court man pressure after dead ball possessions.
- Use trap as directed.
- Use Run and Jump as directed.

A containment press enhances the total defensive effort. It takes time off of the shot clock, and it keeps pressure on their team as they must respect it. This respect is gained by carefully planned and executed traps or run and jump. Letting a point guard bring the ball up the court without any resistance takes the fear factor away and gives the offense an advantage.

****

This defense may appear to be too simple to be good. Simplicity enhances a player's and a team's ability to react. Quick and intelligent reaction is essential to stopping a good opponent. This defense has been proven to be effective. I have used it for over forty years, but many of my assistants and former players turned coaches, have won numerous championships using it.

One aspect of this defense that is overlooked, but tremendously important, is the emphasis of playing defense without fouling. Fouling either puts an opponent into bonus or gives them free throws. An opponent will score more points from free throws then a play, a drive, or any offensive maneuver. Consider this: a 50 percent free throw shooter will score 1 point for every two free throws and a 75 percent free throw shooter will score 1.5 points for every two free throws. Both of these numbers are much more effective than plays, drives, cuts, or screen at ball to name a few. Do not allow your players to foul foolishly for you are asking for defensive problems and probably losses.

The ball line defense is ideal for use in the spaces. In these situations, there is not time to set up; consequently the defensive team will be defending an unpredictable offense. I believe that the principles of the ball line defense make a big difference in the total defense, because so much time in a game is played in unpredictable spaces. Only lately has that made sense to me, after recognizing the impact of spaces.

The spaces create a realistic problem for any defense. It needs to be addressed with some plan; the players can't "be thrown under the bus". I don't believe, though, you can play one defense for the plays and another for the spaces. I think that you need one defense that covers all the situations. The Ball Line defense does that.

CHAPTER TWENTY ONE

TEACHING CONCEPTS FOR THE BALL LINE DEFENSE

It isn't how you teach, but how they learn.

Teaching a rule defense is similar to teaching the Monk offense as it relies heavily on instinctive reactions that have been internalized through repetition and experience. There are three phases of defense which must be considered and learned: half-court defense, full-court defense, and defending the third element. As we have pointed out in previous chapters defending the third element will be the team's biggest challenge. The ball line defense is designed to do just that.

Any type of defensive teaching is hard because the players do not accept it easily. Our society is interested in offense and the players sense this and put their emphasis on it. How many times have you seen players, on their own time, practicing defense? They practice offense. Coaches are not much better; they spend most of their thinking and planning time on offense.

I was an assistant on a NBA team that had three player development coaches and not one of them worked with the players on defense. I brought this up in a coaches meeting and they sheepishly agreed to start working on our defensive needs. It lasted one day, and I never saw a defensive drill again. It is just natural that most players will have the strongest interest in offense, so the challenge for the coach is to overcome this.

Playing defense by rules, as in the ball line defense is relatively simple. Simplicity is important because defense reacts to what the offense dictates. Complexity just clutters the mind and disrupts the necessary instinctive reactions. Both the system and the drills must relate to this simplicity and need to be practiced consistently on a daily basis. The emphasis is on the three pillars of defense, and using simple approaches to the basic structured offensive situations. In the end, the players have to do the playing, so teaching the rules and how to approach the various situations in simple terms will give them some freedom to work from. This is especially important in the spaces when the offensive team is improvising, which in reality is the biggest portion of the game.

The guidelines listed below, if conscientiously applied day after day, will have your team playing solidly and effectively on defense.

TEACHING GUIDLINES

1. The coach must be intensely involved in each aspect of defensive teaching and cannot approach it with a nonchalant attitude. Make defense important to you and the players will respond.
2. Keep the drills simple and focus on one skill until the skill is mastered.
3. If you want players that can contain ball penetration (drives) they must spend considerable time on defensive movement (footwork) and on 1 on 1 play.
4. It is difficult to cover all the situations, especially in scramble, but the players should learn the concepts that apply to these situations. For example, recognizing a screen away, even when it appears in an unusual structure and immediately knowing how to defend it requires well trained instincts.
5. Work on defense at the beginning of practice when the players are fresh. Players tend to work on offense even when they are tired, but defense is laborious and they slack off when tired and their learning is lessened.
6. It is important that players see the entire picture first and understand clearly where the parts fit in. This will make the breakdown drills more relevant.
7. Work on ball containment, shot contesting, and defensive rebounding in some way every day.

BALL LINE DEFENSE DRILLS

Whether you think you can or think you can't, you're right.

Henry Ford

There are many drills for defense. Books and clinics will provide a plethora of them. But drills need to relate to our defense; most defensive drills at clinics relate to nothing. The drills presented in this section relate to the ball line defense, but they are important to defense in general. A great deal of time, effort, and motivation is put into those drills that develop the three pillars of defense: playing a man with the ball, contesting shots, and defensive rebounding.

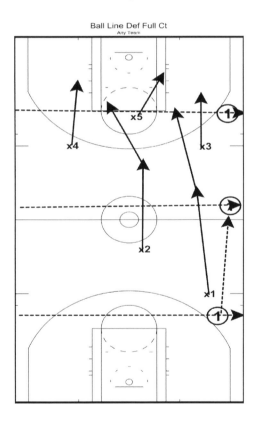

This is not a drill, but we use it the first day to show the ball line positions. Carefully go over each position of the ball and explain the ball line. Then show the defensive positions from each ball line. We emphasize having five defensive men below the ball line. Talk to the players about getting there quickly; slow adjustments away from the ball can create driving holes.

95

SHELL DRILL

This drill is used to show positions in relation to ball and man, moving from overplay position to the sag position and back to overplay, and the position of the defensive man playing the man with the ball. Begin this drill with slow passing and no movement of the offense. In the initial teaching I tell them when to pass—by shouting "Pass" -- to control the drill. It allows time to see where each player is and if he has correct position. Then speed up the passing, add controlled movement as described, and last allow slow drives by the offense. This drill can and should be used with a one guard front also. Keep one team on defense for about 20 seconds. Then the defense becomes offense and offense becomes defense. This is a very important drill and early in the season it should be done every day. Later in the season less use is needed but it should be used all year long.

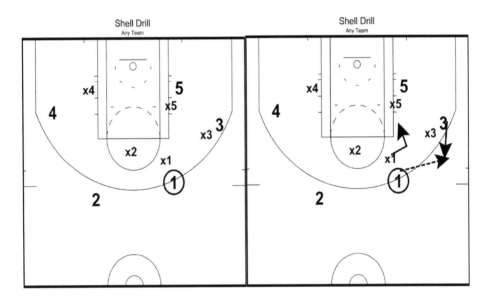

Allow time to go over these positions carefully at first —check and correct. In the Right diagram, after the coach commands "pass" 1 passes to 3 and now all defensive players adjust to the ball and their man.

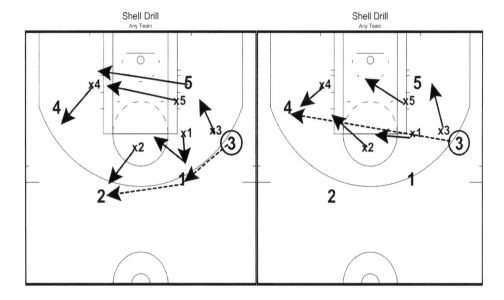

The left frame shows the movement of the ball and the adjustments. These passes are on command from the coach. On each pass the coach should check and correct positions. A difficult adjustment that is usually missed is going from a weak side player to overplay as the ball is swung. Go very slow at first. On the right are shown the adjustments on a cross court pass to the weak side which requires very fast adjustments.

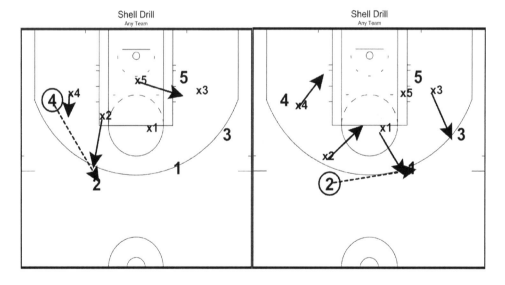

These diagrams show the adjustments on each pass. The post man goes from block to block. At first, disallow passes to the post man until perimeter adjustments are learned.

DEFENSIVE FOOTWORK DRILLS:

I use two defensive footwork drills and rotate them every other practice but one is used every day. The drill in the left frame is diagramed as in the half-court, but it is done using the length of the floor to have more space. In the right diagram the players go two at a time by command of the coach, and when finished form a line on the other side. It is important for the players to learn footwork on both sides of the floor.

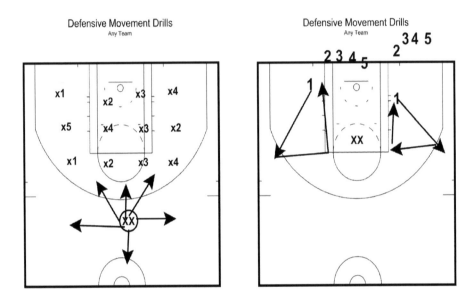

The coach uses hand movements for the drill on the left, making the players slide step sideways, up and back, and diagonal up and back. On the right, when the coach says "go" each player slide steps to free throw line extended, then drops the front foot aggressively to slide step to the lane, then drops the outside foot so he is facing sideline and slide steps in. The players change lines after each trial.

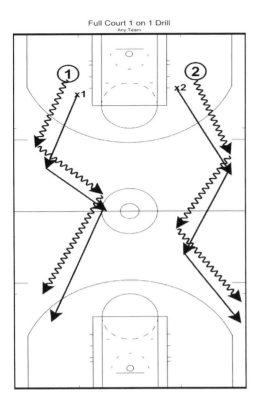

1 VS 1 LENGTH OF THE FLOOR DEFENSIVE DRILL

This full-court drill is our initial ball containment drill. It helps players to learn position on the ball as it is dribbled. Keep the drill slow until they can master the position taught, then allow them to go hard once the dribbler reaches the top of the key on the opposite end. On the other end the players change offense to defense; and defense to offense and come back the other way.

If you have a large group it is ok to use the middle lane. Make the dribbler stay within the lines designated. Have the players change lanes so they are comfortable in any position on the floor.

1 VS 1 HALF COURT DEFENSIVE DRILL

This is a simple 1 on 1 drill that needs to be used often. Because ball containment is so important, this becomes the most important defensive drill in our system. The defensive player overplays his man, but allows the ball in. He then adjusts to get the correct position on the man with the ball. His effort is to control the drive by an imaginary 8' box around the basket. Change offense and defense; change lines.

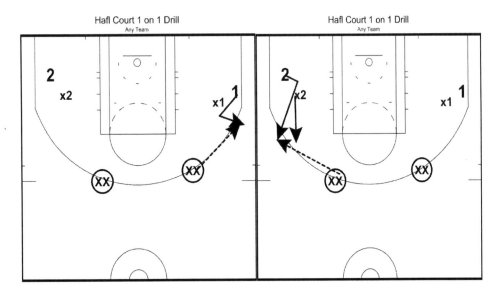

Each coach has a ball and each line goes separately. The diagram on left shows the players that go first, then players in the right diagram go. Then players change offense to defense, defense to offense. They change lines after each set. The coach should make sure it is a strong overplay, but the defender allows the ball in, and then makes a quick adjustment to forcing dribble to the middle. Coaches need to work hard on this drill.

CONTEST THE SHOT DRILL:

Use teams of white and dark in this drill. One team is on defense and has 3 players on the court in positions as shown; extra players are off the court. The other team has four players around the outside as shown. The coach throws the ball to one of the outside players and the drill begins and continues until the offensive team takes a shot. One defensive player must be on the ball. The other two sag on the lane lines. The player on the ball can not follow the pass so he must drop to a sag position shown. The offensive players cannot fake or drive. It is important to teach good contests. A good contest is made by the player going straight up with his hand extended as far as possible and he should contest regardless of how far away he is from the shooter. Defense stays on defense for about 3 minutes but rotates players after a shot or turnover. Then they change to offense and the outside team becomes defense. This drill simulates scramble. If this drill is run almost daily, you will get strong results in the game.

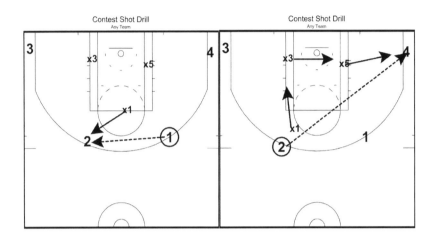

Left: x1 takes first pass. Right: x1 cannot follow the pass and drops to sag position, x3 moves to ball side. X5 must cover that pass.

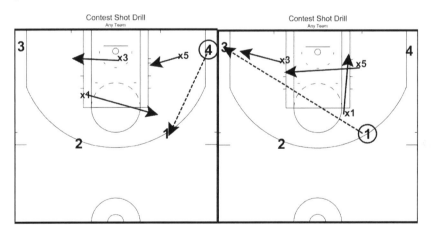

On pass out from corner either x1 or x3 could take it. On right: the cross court pass is covered by x3, x1 drops back to sag position, x5 adjusts.

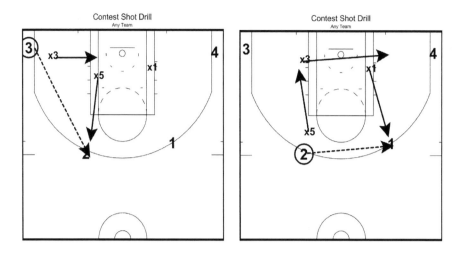

These two diagrams show the correct shifts and responsibilities.

The contest the shot drill is very important to the ball line defense. It must be reviewed all season. This is the only drill used for contesting the shot, but if used correctly you will see a significant improvement in lowering your opponents shooting percentage. Once the players have learned the drill it needs to only be used a short time each day. It is more important to be used consistently all year long.

DEFENSIVE REBOUNDING PRINCIPLES

In the Monk system defensive rebounding is taught differently. We do not teach blocking out. Blocking out prohibits a rebounder from pursuit of the ball; the only rebounds they get are those that come right to them. Instead, players are told to just screen their man (or any man), quickly establish a good position on the basket, watch the flight of the ball, and pursue the ball when it comes off the basket. Pursuit is the key, and emphasize going after the ball wherever it goes and stress this in the drills.

It is important to understand clearly each of these four principles:

1. **SCREEN YOUR MAN:** It is not necessary to physically restrain your man (or any man) but a quick screen to delay his direct move to the basket is

all that is necessary. Do not attempt to make contact with him. However don't get pushed from your position either.

2. **POSITION ON THE BASKET:** This is more important than stopping your opponent from rebounding. Your position will vary according to where you are at the time of the shot. If you are outside, you should fight to get around the free throw line area for long rebounds. Those close to the basket should get a position at least three feet from the basket so you are free to pursue all rebounds. This position may require physical play to keep from getting pushed into a position too close to the basket. These positions are important.

3. **FOLLOW THE FLIGHT OF THE BALL:** Many players turn and look at the rim, in fact some coaches teach this. But, watching the rim without watching the ball gives little time to learn where the rebound may go. Sensing the direction of the rebound is essential to pursuit. Do not take this principle lightly and establish in your players the habit of doing it.

4. **PURSUE THE BALL:** Go for every ball, wherever it goes. A large majority of rebounds are obtained off the floor and from bobbles. A team trained to pursue the ball gets those rebounds. When five players are in good position and pursue every rebound, size is no longer a factor.

Defensive rebounding requires aggressiveness and quickness; coaches must work hard in this area. In the Monk system we put a lot of attention on the four principles stated above and practices include work on this skill as a team every day. Instill in your players this relentless pursuit of every rebound until it is embedded into their instincts. Help them realize that rebounds picked off of the floor are as valuable as those captured off of the basket.

DEFENSIVE REBOUNDING DRILL:

The purpose of this drill is to teach players the four principles of defensive rebounding: screen your man, quickly get correct position on the basket, watch the flight of the ball, and pursue the ball. All five players go for the ball. After a few sessions we use this drill to start our fast break as shown in the fast break section.

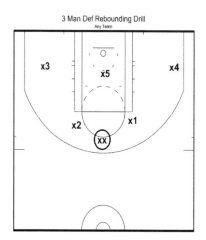

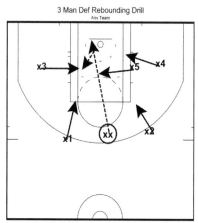

On the left is the starting positions; players face coach and he will start the drill by swinging the ball and the players defensive slide according to his motion. On the right the coach shoots and the players use the four defensive rebounding principles. The coach must be alert to instruct these principles.

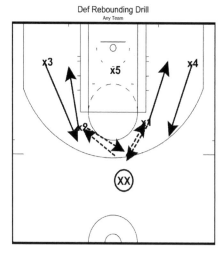

This drill is used after the drill above is well learned and players have developed the habits of the four principles. Now the coach will pass to one player and he passes back and exchanges with player below. At the same time, the coach throws to the player on the other side and he does the same. When the coach has them in new positions, he shoots and they adjust their rebounding responsibilities.

The five man rebounding drill diagramed above is a good way to teach team rebounding principles. The next drill—3 men rebounding drill—teaches pursuit. This drill also teaches aggressiveness, and good monitoring by the coach is necessary.

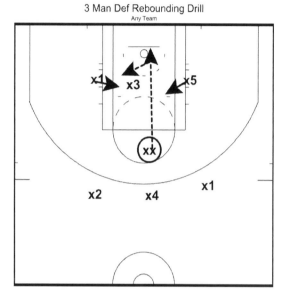

3 Man Def Rebounding Drill
Any Team

3 players are competing against each other for the defensive rebound. The drill does not end until one player secures it. Anything goes except players can not block out, or push a player but as long as they are going for the ball everything else is o.k. There is no out of bounds and players must continue to pursue wherever the ball goes, even into the stands. The one who secures it gets to stay in. The other two players are replaced by new ones from the lines. If a player gets three in a row, he is excused from the drill for that day.

INTRODUCTORY SCREEN AT BALL DRILL:

This drill introduces the coordination between the defensive man on the screener and the defensive man on the ball. This is the only drill we use to defend the screen at the ball. It is simple and it keeps the defense intact. The key skill is going under the screen quickly and aggressively. The player guarding the screener must step back to provide a space for the player guarding the ball to get through. Some teams will roll the screener into the man trying to go under (this is a violation but hardly ever called, so players must learn how to handle it). When the screener uses this maneuver, there is a space to go over the top which is acceptable and in this drill the player on the ball gets comfortable with doing this. Players have to learn both skills; how to go under with skill and quickness, or reacting to the space and going over the top quickly. Competence in this skill avoids rotating, which keeps the defensive team out of scramble. By relying only on this skill of going under we make the offensive team beat us at the screen and we stay intact because we don't need to rotate.

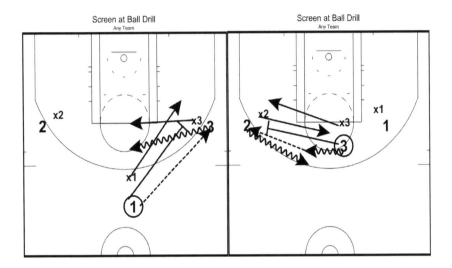

Number 1 starts the drill by passing to 3 and he follows his pass to set a screen on 3's man, x1 loosens up and x3 goes under the screen. 3 dribbles to the middle of the court and passes to 2 and follows his pass to set a screen on 2's man. This continues until the coach stops the drill and changes offense to defense, defense to offense. After the players have mastered this simple drill, the offensive players are allowed to attempt to score but stay in this drill until they get an opportunity. Don't let them get out of control and don't let them dispense with the use of screens.

SCREEN DOWN DEFENSE:

The Screen Down (or Pin Down) is a well used offensive maneuver, so it is important to have a well established defensive plan for it. From the offensive teaching we learned earlier, we know there are five ways a cutter may use the screen and we also know that a well drilled team will have equally as many moves for the screener. It is impossible to have a fool proof method of defending each of them, but our principles will defeat four of them: the wing cut, back-cut, curl, and baby curl. Our weakness is the flare to the corner, but that shot, generally, is also a weakness of the offensive player.

Our rule is to go ball-side of the screen and this defends well the four stunts mentioned above. But going ball-side requires skill and that requires repetitious practice with alert coaching to make proper corrections. It is important to learn to recognize the ball-side of all screens away from the ball, as they can materialize in different angles, distance, and with different players. But careful adherence to the rule for these screens will negate their effectiveness.

Handling the flare is difficult but the shot obtained from this move is also difficult, as the player is sharply going away from the basket and has poor vision. However, there are some players that can make that shot so we must be prepared. If the defensive player maintains physical contact with the cutter, he can sometimes feel that the player will make that move and then he disregards the rule of going ball side. With some players that move is predictable (that is they do it all the time) so the rule is ignored and the defensive player chases him to the corner or where the flare takes him.

This simple drill teaches the concepts well but it must be practiced consistently and enthusiastically, by the coach as well as the players.

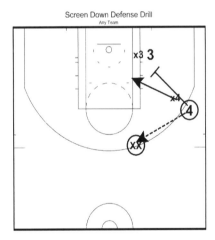

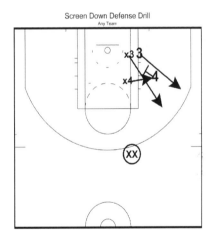

This drill should have two lines; one on the baseline and one at the wing. The wing player has the ball and throws to the coach and immediately goes down to set a screen. X4 may hold him up but does not get out of position because he has to loosen up at the point of the screen. X3 gets the position shown and this takes away the back-cut. When the cutter cuts toward the wing x3 goes ball side as shown and this stops the curl and the baby curl. To introduce this drill have the players walk through this maneuver a number of times until they are confident of it. Then the drill should be done live with one rule and that is that the screen down must be done first every time, after that the drill is live.

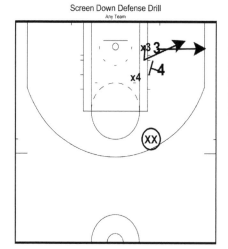

Screen Down Defense Drill
Any Team

This is how the flare should be defended if the defensive player suspects or knows the offensive player is going to the corner. X3 sometimes can feel the flare coming if he maintains physical contact with the cutter.

SCREEN AWAY DEFENSE DRILL:

To continue with the concepts of defending screening situations that do not involve the ball, we use a particularly difficult offensive situation which is the weak side back screen for a weak side cutter. We practice against this type of situation because it is used in a variety of ways. We have designed a simple continuity offense that allows for effective practice on this troublesome offensive maneuver. The continuity is diagramed and should be mastered first without defense. Depending on the skill level of the players, competence in running it should not take long. Walk through it first, and then speed up without taking shots.

When defense is added they should walk through it first, and for some time. This is coaching and learning time. It should not be hurried After the coach is sure that all players know what to do, the drill can be live, but be careful that the players run the offense to get their shots or drives. Exchange offense and defense after every possession. Be prepared to run this for many practices before it becomes effective, but when it does it is a wonderful drill that prepares players to defend most screening situations away from the ball. The coach must be very alert to make corrections because the players will get confused—at least early on.

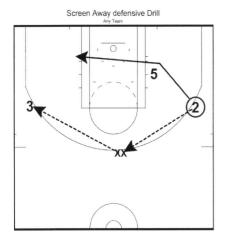

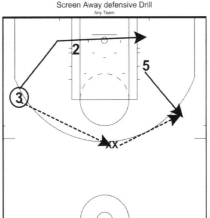

Wing player 2 has the ball and starts the continuity by passing to the coach who passes to opposite wing player. At the same time, 2 walks his man into the screen and cuts baseline. He is now the post-up player. 3 passes back to the coach who passes to 5 breaking out to the wing and 3 makes the baseline cut. Players do not shoot, they just pass and cut.

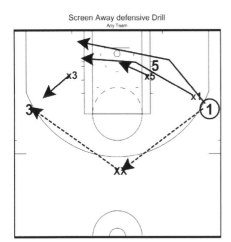

When defense is added the players should walk through the assignments before it goes live. When the ball is swung to the weak side, the wing defender and the post defender move to a sag position. When 1 makes his cut x1 goes ball side regardless of what the cutter does. He should be taught to make this move over the screen quickly to get back to his man as soon as possible. The defender guarding the screener takes a sag position off his man and this puts him into good position to help on the cutter. Once the cut is made and new positions obtained, the ball is swung again and the drill continues. Each defender will have to play the cutter once and the screener once. Continue to walk thru it until all players can do it. When the drill is run live, make sure the offensive team runs the offense.

109

DEFENSE ON UCLA CUT AND SCREEN DOWN DRILL:

On this drill the defensive players work against a back pick and a screen down. The cutter's defensive player goes ball side regardless of which side the cutter goes and the screener's man loosens up to help on the cutter. The cutter's defender must be quick to get back to his man. If his man stays ball side he will need to overplay the post-up pass. The drill continues and if the ball is thrown to the high-post player the defensive player on the wing will have to defend the screen down. This drill will challenge your best defensive players. Players rotate around to play all three positions defensively and offensively. The defender must learn to play against a back screen and this drill will help. Be forewarned that this drill will take a few practices before players can do it well.

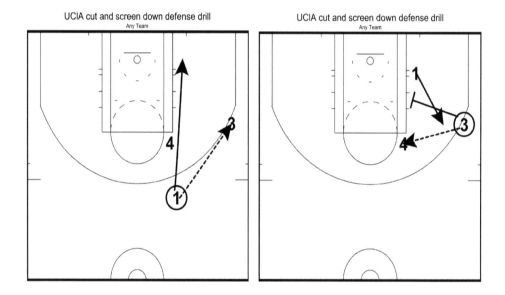

UCIA cut and screen down defense drill
Any Team

UCIA cut and screen down defense drill
Any Team

This is a simple offensive set, but used quite a bit. The diagram should be self explanatory but make sure players can run it well before adding defense.

UCIA cut and screen down defense drill
Any Team

UCIA cut and screen down defense drill
Any Team

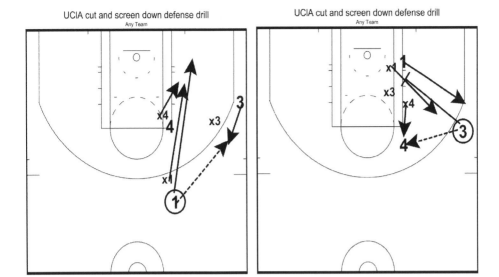

On the pass from 1 to 3 the defender on 1 drops to ball line which puts him in a good position to go ball side of screen. The screener's man must give ground to help on the cutter if he goes on the opposite side of the screen. This fits the rule as the non-penetrating passes are not overplayed. The cutter's defender must get back to his man quickly. As soon as he recognizes the screen down he will have to adjust. The screen down is managed as in the previous screen down drill.

SUMMARY

In order to have a strong team defense, it must be able to play against a predictable offense and an unpredictable offense. It has to be able to perform when it is scrambled as well as when it is set We know this because it has been shown that playing in the spaces is the most productive area for any offense. The Ball Line principles (rules) and positions protect the defense from becoming scrambled, but should they become scrambled, its rules maintain the defense.

Defense is hard to perfect. Players will ignore it. It is hard work with little prestige or reward. There is little glory in playing defense well but to win consistently it has to be addressed and mastered. There is no other aspect of basketball that will define the coach as well as his ability to teach and perfect defense.

The coach will determine the success or failure of the ball line defense. Any defense requires a tenacious work ethic and the ball line defense is no exception. There is only one way this defense will fail, and that is if the coach does not study it, commit to it, and motivate players to perfect it

It starts with practice. The drills shown have proven they work; use them and stick to them. Use the principles and the rules without exception, and do not compromise your belief and your faith. The players will resist the work involved to play good defense but don't give in to them. Instead, work with them and they will eventually respond if they know the coach is committed.

The best practice for defense is 4 versus 4, and 5 versus 5 against the Monk offense. It will develop all the skills required.

Master the Three Pillars of Defense which are contain the ball, contest shots, and rebound, and you can play with anyone, anyplace.

CHAPTER TWENTY TWO

ROVER ZONE DEFENSE

A certain amount of opposition is a great help to a person. Kites rise against, not with the wind.

John Neal

As a rule, I do not play a lot of zone defense. However, I have found it to be helpful at times; in fact, it has led to a lot of wins. In our system, it is not used as a primary defense, but as a supplemental defense. The zone we use in the Monk System is called the Rover Zone. It appears to be a 1-2-2, but it has shifts that are different than a regular 1-2-2. The role of the Rover makes this zone unique.

The basic shifts are shown in the following three pages, with explanations. These shifts are quite easy, but they do not cover everything that can happen in a game. So we rely on certain rules that cover the situations that can occur. It requires practice to learn the difference of playing a zone rather than a man-to-man defense. Before we go into the general rules, it is important to understand the role of the Rover. Also, it is vital that all players are able to play the Rover position. The defense at times dictates rotating various players as Rovers.

ROVER POSITION

The Rover position is simple, but does require energy and endurance. There is only one rule: maintain a position in a direct line with the ball and the basket. Coaches need to take the time to show the entire team where these positions are. It is very simple, but do not take it for granted that the players understand; show them.

The Rover's position stops passes and drives into the middle of the zone.

This gives the zone a strong advantage over other zones. It literally stops penetration of the zone by driving. By having this element eliminated, the other four players are in excellent position to defend outside players.

Any type of player can play the Rover but, if possible, a taller player that has quickness can be helpful, especially in rebounding. The main ingredient is quickness and aggressiveness. The Rover spends a lot of time chasing the ball, and this requires energy. It is important the players clearly understand the correct position of the Rover, in relation to the ball. There is a tendency for players not to get deep enough when the ball is in the corner. It takes time for the Rover to gain confidence that he can play this deep and handle the pass to the top of the key.

GENERAL RULES AND ADJUSTMENTS

- Play the man with the ball a little looser to help make the shift after a pass easier and quicker.
- Aggressively contest all shots.
- In a screen at the ball situation, the man guarding the ball should always go over the top.
- Always be alert for cutters from the top and the weak side.
- When releasing a cutter leaving a zone, communicate to the player whose zone is receiving the cutter.
- Team rebounding is a must; go aggressively to the ball—every ball.
- If the man with the ball drives—play normal man-to-man defense until driver is stopped by the Rover.
- On skip, swing, or cross-court passes chase the ball but be alert for cutters.

ZONE POSITIONS AND ADJUSTMENTS

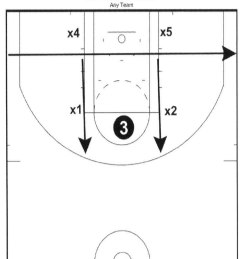

These are the starting positions of the Rover zone defense, and the zone areas that each player is responsible for. 3 in the dark circle is the Rover.

These three positions show how the Rover lines up with the ball and the basket. The Rover always stays on the lane lines or there about.

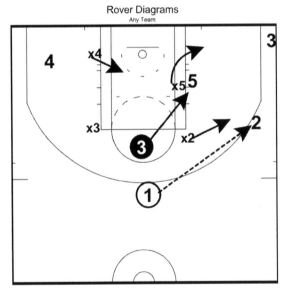

Rover Diagrams
Any Team

These are the starting positions for the Rover zone when the ball is in the middle at the top. Number three in Black Circle is the Rover. When the ball is at the top middle x4 and x5 must deny the pass to any player in the low post position.

Rover Diagrams
Any Team

When the ball is at the wing, the Rover quickly moves to a position in direct line between the ball and the basket. X5 can now move off the overplay position on 5. The Rover can stop passes to the post up.

If the ball is in the corner x5 or x4 must cover that man. The Rover position is in line with the ball. He must be careful not to get behind a man, but on the side so he prohibits a pass in that area. X3 and x4 are alert for cutters into their zones. X2 drops into the position shown to help on passes and cutters into that area.

The pass from the deep corner to the top of the circle is a problem. If the Rover cannot get back to top of the circle from his deep position it requires the weak side free throw line man (x1) to take the Rover's zone, and the Rover replaces him.

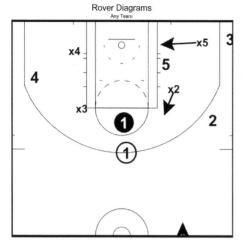

X1 now becomes the Rover and the original Rover becomes the wing zone player.

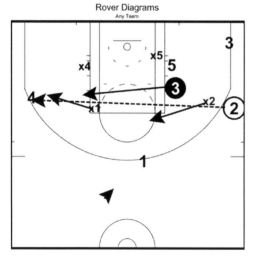

The cross court pass is handled as shown. The Rover must make a quick recovery to the other side and take up his position. In this drawing either x1 or x4 could take the ball depending on how deep the weak side offensive player is positioned.

ROVER ZONE SUMMARY

The diagrams show the basic movement of the defensive players in the Rover zone. If the offensive team uses movement, the zone must be very alert and aggressive to follow the rules. The only way to master these moves is to practice and play the zone a lot. Remember the Rover discourages and prohibits drives, which makes the offense play around the outside.

There are a couple of precautions I would like to make a coach aware of. When the ball is at the top of the key and played by the Rover, it is important that the deep players position themselves so a direct pass to their areas cannot be made. This is a strong concern because if the ball can be passed directly from the top, it is very hard to defend or give help.

Another situation that requires explanation is that there is an area between the deep man and the wing man that is vague and leaves both players uncertain of who covers him. The best rule is if there is doubt, the wing man should cover but make sure the wing does not go too deep or a driving hole will be opened.

This is not a complicated defense but it does require practice and instruction. Once mastered it can be a strong tool in the total defensive package. Study the preceding diagrams, and practice, practice, practice.

CHAPTER TWENTY THREE

PRACTICE PLANNING

The pessimist complains about the wind; the optimist expects it to change; the realist adjusts the sails.

William Arthur Ward

The team that practices well plays well. With over thirty years as a head coach, I can honestly say that there have been few practices that were not planned. I have boxes of practice notebooks in my home that will prove this. In these notebooks I have kept every practice in my coaching career. There has been nothing more valuable for me, in my coaching life, than learning to plan good practices.

If you spend less than an hour planning a practice you are doing a disservice to your team. I allow two hours for planning before every practice. Each coach has their own way of doing it, but I don't know any good ones that ignore planning.

You may have your own way, but in this chapter I will give you my way of planning as a guide for those that have not developed a method. Be warned that there are coaches who scoff at planning practices. They even brag about running their practices without a plan. I have heard all of that. My experience has been that those coaches have bad practices.

My method is to formulate a master plan for pre-season and training camp practices. I make a list of all the areas that our team needs. I then plot on the master plan when I will introduce each item to the team. I follow an appropriate progression and allow ample time to master each step of the progression. In this way, I assure myself that the important areas will be properly practiced before we begin playing games.

I use a specific mental procedure in my planning. It goes like this. I ask myself if I could only teach one thing on offense what it would be. When I make that decision I insert it into the plan. Next, I ask myself if I could only choose two things what would be second. I continue this mental exercise until I have all offensive areas in my plan. Then I do the same with defense. By doing this, I am certain that the most important areas are taught first and have the time allotted to do them well. There are always things I cannot get in before the first game, but I know the most important areas have been practiced. Those I can't get in will not be needed in all probability.

Every year there are timing adjustments. I may have allowed only three days for learning a part of our system, but as it turns out it requires four days. I then adjust the master plan accordingly. Like any coach, I go into the first game feeling that the team is not ready, but I am confident I have the important things ready.

On the following page I show an example of a master plan. This is an actual plan that I prepared for a professional team that I was to coach. It is a normal plan and is prepared each season. From this master plan I prepare each practice. As you can see on the master plan I estimated the minutes for each item. I may adjust the minutes in the daily practice plan, but the total minutes remain the same.

Daily or individual practice plans are covered in the next chapter. Before leaving the master plan I would like to point out that there may be times I need a master plan during the season. For example, if we have a short break from games during the season, I may make a master plan for these days. Also, if we were preparing for a tournament or play-offs, I always did a master plan to ensure we prepared correctly.

I do not use a master plan once we start to play games. Each practice is then dictated by our needs at the time. As the season progresses, we learn what areas the team is weak and strong in. As these become evident, we plan accordingly for each practice.

Practices 1-7	Practices 8-14	Practices 15-21	Practices 21-28
Non-Contact 560 Minutes (80)	**Non-Contact 560 Minutes (80)**	**Non-Contact 560 Minutes (80)**	**Non-Contact 560 Minutes (80)**
Stretch **Def Footwork** **Off w/o Defense** **Conditioning** **TBD**	**Stretch** **Def Footwork** **Off w/o Defense** **Conditioning** **TBD**	**Stretch** **Def Footwork** **Off w/o Defense** **Conditioning** **TBD**	**Stretch** **Def Footwork** **Off w/o Defense** **Conditioning** **TBD**
DEFENSE: 448 Min (64)	**DEFENSE: 448 Min (64)**	**DEFENSE: 448 Min (64)**	**DEFENSE: 448 Min (64)**
Man to Man: **Shell Drill** **Contest the Shot** **1 on 1 Defense** **Overplay Wing** **Post Up Def** **Shot Blocking** **Vs. No Play--Free Lance** **Weak side to Strong side Cuts** **Basket Cuts from Top** **Def Rebounding**	**Man to Man:** **Repeat Wk One Drills** **Mid and Side S/R's** **Screen Down Def** **HP Cut w/screen Def** **Hawk Cut Def** **Princeton Hand Off Def Drill** **Intro FB Def**	**Man to Man:** **Continue Drills and Situations** **Floppy Defense** **Intro Rover Zone** **Shell Drill** **Vs. Monk** **End of Quarter Def**	**Man to Man Cont.** **Rover Zone** **Intro Man to Man to Rover** **End of Game Situations**
OFFENSE: 672 Min (96)	**OFFENSE: 672 Min (96)**	**OFFENSE: 672 Min (96)**	**OFFENSE: 672 Min (96)**

Monk Offense--W and W/O Def
  Screen Down Cuts/Shots
  Screen Away Cuts/Shots
  Top Cuts
 	
  Split Cuts
  4 on 4 --- 5 on 5
 	
Cut Offense--W/ and W/O Def
  Cut One
 	
  5 on 5
 	
Scrimmage -- 15 Min
 	
Fast Break
  Shell w/o def
 	
  Def Reb Break
  Wing Cross on Made
  FB to Monk
	Monk Offense--Cont.
	
	  Repeat Drills
	
	Cut Offense--Cont.
	
	  Intro Cut Two
	  Intro Automatic
	
	Intro 1 Go To Play
	Controlled Full Court w/offenses
	
	Scrimmage 20 Min
	Fast Break
	  Week One Cont
	
	  Wing Cross to Cut
		Monk Offense -- Continued
		
		Cut Offense-- Continued
		  Into Cut 3 and Swing
		  Into Cut Go To Play
		
		Controlled Full Court Cont
		Scrimmage Continued
		
		Into Side and End Out of Bounds
		
		Fast Break Continued
			Monk Offense Continued
			Cut Offense Continued
			
			FB Continued
			
			Into 3rd Go To Play
			
			Into End of Game Plays
			
			Live Work Continued as needed
			
			Late Game Situations

CHAPTER TWENTY FOUR

FIRST TWELVE PRACTICE PLANS

Ninety percent of what you learn is in the beginning.

The daily practice plan should have a definite format that is used for each practice. It should include the date, and the number of the practice. Allow enough room to put the time that each item or drill is to start and how long it will last. The name of the item or drill needs to be included. Also, it is helpful to your support staff if the equipment needed for each drill is listed.

The next page shows the format we used and how we stated the items. Of course, there can be many varieties of form, but this form was simple and complete. Copies were made for all coaches and support staff. There was one copy that we placed on the scoring table. The first thirty minutes were the same for each practice. We did rotate the two shooting drills and the two defensive slide drills each day. This was consistent. The other thing that was consistent was placing all the defensive drills first. I have always wanted the defensive drills to be when the players were fresh. Offensive play is more pleasurable and players will continue to work hard even when they are tired. All of our live team drills and scrimmages came last in the practice. In early practices we had a definite conditioning program, and this was done at the end of practice.

I try to stay with a 2 hour practice. I insisted that the players were on time for practice and I felt it only fair that I was on time dismissing them.

Practice time for each drill or team play should be short. I use 15 – 20 minutes the first day of a new drill, but reduce to 10 to 15 minutes after the first day. As the players become more skilled, these times went down. Do not make practices punishment. That is sending the wrong message to the players. Practicing and playing should not be drudgery. It may be hard, but shorter periods of time for each drill make it less burdensome.

Oct 19,2011   NUMBER: 23

TIME	PRACTICE ITEM	EQUIPMENT
10:00	Talk	X
10:05	Shooting #1	8 Balls, Clock
10:15	Stretch	X
10:25	Slide Drill #1	X
10:30	Shot Blocking Drill	1 Ball
10:40	5 Man Rebounding Drill	1 Ball
10:50	5 vs. 5 L/F	1 Ball
11:00	2 Man FB Drill	5 Balls
11:10	Screen Down Drill	3 Balls
11:20	Cut 1 Off w/o Def	2 Balls
11:25	Cut 1 Off w/ Def	1 Ball
11:40	5 vs. 5 Monk and FC	1 Ball

COMMENTS:

FIRST TWELVE PRATICES

INTRODUCING THE MONK SYSTEM

The next pages of twelve practice plans comprise the initial practices in developing the Monk system. I have included them so a coach has a format that he or she can follow to accurately begin the training method endorsed in this book.

I have always followed the progression that is displayed in these plans. There were times I may make minor adjustments to fit the situation, but I stayed true to this approach. For the coach that has determined he or she is committed to the Monk method, these practices should be followed faithfully. It is important that the coach new to this system uses it as it is written in the same way a careful cook follows a recipe.

The drills used have been described in previous pages, and are all in the coach's book that is also presented.

TIME	PRACTICE ITEM	EQUIPMENT
3:00	Talk	X
3:05	Shooting #1	8 Balls, Cl
3:20	Stretch	X
3:35	Slide Drill #1	X
3:40	Shell Drill	1 Ball
4:00	5 Man Rebounding Drill	2 Balls
4:10	5 Man Fast Break	2 Balls
4:20	Monk Offense	2 Balls
4:40	Screen Away Drill	3 Balls
4:55	Conditioning 6	Clock

COMMENTS:

Extra time was allowed for each drill because it was the first time seeing it. Conditioning was timed wind sprints the length of the floor. Players must do in 30 seconds.

TIME	PRACTICE ITEM	EQUIPMENT
3:00	Talk	X
3:05	Shooting #2	8 Balls, Cl
3:20	Stretch	X
3:35	Slide Drill #2	X
3:40	Shell Drill	1 Ball
4:00	5 Man Rebounding Drill	2 Balls
4:10	5 Man Fast Break	2 Balls
4:20	Monk Offense	2 Balls
4:40	Screen Away Drill	3 Balls
4:55	Conditioning 6	Clock

COMMENTS:

This is same practice as #1 except Shooting and Slide Drill. These are foundation drills and system drills. We wanted to make sure we had enough time.

TIME	PRACTICE ITEM	EQUIPMENT
3:00	Talk	X
3:05	Shooting #1	8 Balls, Cl
3:15	Stretch	X
3:25	Slide Drill #1	X
3:30	Shell Drill	1 Ball
3:45	1 vs. 1 L/F Drill	2 Balls
4:00	5 Man Reb Drill	2 Balls
4:05	5 Man FB Drill	2 Balls
4:15	Screen Away Drill	3 Balls
4:25	Monk Offense w/o Def	2 Balls
4:35	4 vs. 4 Drill Half Ct	2Balls/Clock
4:50	Conditioning 7	Clock

COMMENTS:

Most repeated drills were shortened as the players required less instruction. Two new drills were introduced. Conditioning is increased by 1 every two days.

TIME	PRACTICE ITEM	EQUIPMENT
3:00	Talk	X
3:05	Shooting #2	8 Balls, Clock
3:15	Stretch	X
3:25	Slide Drill #2	X
3:30	Shell Drill	1 Ball
3:45	1 vs. 1 L/F Drill	3 Balls
3:55	2 vs. 2 Overplay Drill	1 Ball
4:10	5 Man FB to Monk	2 Balls
4:25	Screen Down Drill	3 Balls
4:40	Monk Offense w/o Def	2 Balls
4:45	4 vs. 4 Drill Half Court	2 Balls/Clock
4:55	Conditioning 7	Clock

COMMENTS:

One new defensive drill; 1 new offensive FB drill added going to Monk offense.

TIME	PRACTICE ITEM	EQUIPMENT
3:00	Talk	X
3:05	Shooting #1	8 Balls, Clock
3:15	Stretch	X
3:25	Slide Drill #1	X
3:30	1 vs. 1 L/F Drill	3 Balls
3:40	2 vs. 2 Overplay Drill	2 Balls
3:55	5 vs. 5 L/F Def Drill	1 Ball
4:05	5 Man FB to Monk	2 Balls
4:15	Screen Down Drill	3 Balls
4:25	Monk Offense w/ Def	1 Ball/Clock
4:40	Scrimmage	1 Ball/Clock
4:55	Conditioning 8	Clock

COMMENTS:

1 new defensive drill added. Used Monk offense vs. def. for 1st time. Used scrimmage to use offense and defense full court. This will always look bad.

TIME	PRACTICE ITEM	EQUIPMENT
3:00	Talk	X
3:05	Shooting #2	8 Balls, Clock
3:15	Stretch	X
3:25	Slide Drill #2	X
3:30	1 vs. 1 L/F Half Court	2 Balls
3:40	2 vs. 2 Overplay Drill	2 Balls
3:50	5 vs. 5 L/F Def Drill	1 Ball
4:05	5 Man FB to Monk	2 Balls
4:15	Back Cut Drills	3 Balls
4:25	Screen Down Drill	3 Balls
4:35	Screen Away Drill	3 Balls
4:40	4 vs. 4 FC Half Ct/Full Ct Drill	1 Ball/Clock
4:55	Conditioning 8	Clock

COMMENTS:

Back cut drill is new. This practice was a repetition of most drills learned to this time. We go up 11 in conditioning and then come back to 9; then we stop conditioning.

TIME	PRACTICE ITEM	EQUIPMENT
3:00	Talk	X
3:05	Shooting #1	8 Balls, Clock
3:15	Stretch	X
3:25	Slide Drill #1	X
3:30	Shell Drill	1 Ball
3:40	2 vs. 2 Overplay Drill	2 Balls
3:50	4 vs. 4 Def Drill	1 Ball/Clock
4:05	Back Cut Drills	3 Balls
4:15	Screen Down Drill	3 Balls
4:20	2 vs. 2 Wing Entry Drill	2 Balls
4:30	Monk Offense w/o Def	2 Balls
4:35	4 vs. 4 FC Half Ct/Full Ct Drill	1 Ball/Clock
4:55	Conditioning 9	Clock

COMMENTS:
Normal progression in this practice.

TIME	PRACTICE ITEM	EQUIPMENT
3:00	Talk	X
3:05	Shooting #2	8 Balls, Clock
3:15	Stretch	X
3:25	Slide Drill #2	X
3:30	Shell Drill	1 Ball
3:40	1 vs. 1 Half Ct Drill	2 Balls
3:50	Contest the Shot Drill	1 Ball
4:05	5 Man FB to Monk	2 Balls
4:15	Screen Down Drill	3 Balls
4:25	Screen Away Drill	3 Balls
4:30	Monk Offense w/o Def	2 Balls
4:35	4 vs. 4 FC Half Ct/Full Ct Drill	1 Ball/Clock
4:55	Conditioning 9	Clock

COMMENTS:

Added Contest the Shot drill. Using a lot of 4 vs. 4 half ct. full ct.

TIME	PRACTICE ITEM	EQUIPMENT
3:00	Talk	X
3:05	Shooting #1	8 Balls, Clock
3:15	Stretch	X
3:25	Slide Drill #1	X
3:30	Shell Drill	1 Ball
3:40	Contest the Shot Drill	1 Ball
3:50	2 vs. 2 O/P Drill	2 Balls
4:05	5 Man FB to Monk	2 Balls
4:15	Screen Down Drill	3 Balls
4:25	Screen Away Drill	3 Balls
4:30	Monk Offense w/o Def	2 Balls
4:35	5 vs. 5 FC Half Ct/Full Ct Drill	1 Ball/Clock
4:55	Conditioning 10	Clock

COMMENTS:

Conditioning level is very high. This is a demanding practice with 20 min. of 5 vs. 5 followed by 10 wind sprints.

TIME	PRACTICE ITEM	EQUIPMENT
3:00	Talk	X
3:05	Shooting #2	8 Balls, Clock
3:15	Stretch	X
3:25	Slide Drill #2	X
3:30	Shell Drill	1 Ball
3:40	Contest the Shot Drill	1 Ball
3:50	1 vs. 1 Full Court Def Drill	3 Balls
4:05	5 Man FB to Monk	2 Balls
4:15	Split Drill	3 Balls
4:30	Screen Away Drill	3 Balls
4:40	Monk Offense w/o Def	2 Balls
4:35	4 vs. 4 FC Half Ct/Full Ct Drill	1 Ball/Clock
4:55	Conditioning 10	Clock

COMMENTS:
Added Split drill. There is quite a bit of the offense and defense drills added; now it is repeated until perfected and internalized.

TIME	PRACTICE ITEM	EQUIPMENT
3:00	Talk	X
3:05	Shooting #1	8 Balls, Clock
3:15	Stretch	X
3:25	Slide Drill #1	X
3:30	1 vs. 1 Half Ct Def Drill	2 Balls
3:40	Contest the Shot Drill	1 Ball
3:50	5 vs. 5 F/C Def Drill	1 Ball/Clock
4:05	5 Man FB to Monk	2 Balls
4:15	Split Drill	3 Balls
4:30	Screen Away Drill	3 Balls
4:40	Monk Offense w/o Def	2 Balls
4:35	5 vs. 5 FC Half Ct/Full Ct Drill	1 Ball/Clock
4:55	Conditioning 11	Clock

COMMENTS:

With a pro team or returning players I would have put in the set offense by now. With inexperienced players it is best to go slow.

TIME	PRACTICE ITEM	EQUIPMENT
3:00	Talk	X
3:05	Shooting #2	8 Balls, Clock
3:15	Stretch	X
3:25	Slide Drill #2	X
3:30	1 vs. 1 Half Ct Def Drill	2 Balls
3:40	Contest the Shot Drill	1 Ball
3:50	2 vs. 2 O/P Drill	2 Balls
4:00	5 Man FB to Monk	2 Balls
4:10	Split Drill	3 Balls
4:20	Back Cut Drill	3 Balls
4:30	Monk Offense w/o Def	2 Balls
4:40	5 vs. 5 FC Half Ct/Full Ct Drill	1 Ball/Clock
4:55	Conditioning 11	Clock

COMMENTS:

At this point, if these 12 practices were followed, the team has been prepared well and has a solid foundation established. All of these drills and following drills are in the coaches book.

CHAPTER TWENTY FIVE

MONK SYSTEM BOOK OF DRILLS

On this page is a complete list of all the drills used to perfect the Monk system. It includes drills that are not in the book. These drills are not necessary for the teaching of the system. It is my intention to develop another book of just the drills with detailed instructions.

DEFENSE

SHELL DRILL

5 ON 5 LENGTH OF FLOOR

1 ON 1 LENGTH OF FLOOR

1 ON 1 DEF DRILL HALF COURT

2 ON 2 OVER PLAY DRILL

5 MAN REBOUNDING DRILL

CONTEST THE SHOT DRILL

SHOT BLOCKING DRILL

FAST BREAK DEF DRILL

SCREEN DOWN DEF DRILL

4 ON 4 DEF DRILL

SCREEN AWAY DEF DRILL

FAST BREAK

2 MAN FAST BREAK DRILL

5 MAN FAST BREAK TO MONK OFFENSE

OFFENSE

MONK OFF W/O DEFENSE

5 VS 5 WITH MONK OFFENSE: HALF AND FULL

SCREEN AWAY DRILL W/O DEFENSE

SCREEN DOWN DRILL W/O DEFENSE

SPLIT DRILL W/O DEFENSE

CUT DRILL FROM THE TOP

CUT DRILL FROM THE WEAKSIDE

BACK CUT DRILLS: TOP AND WING

4 VS 4 WITH MONK OFFENSE: HALF AND FULL

CUT 1 OFFENSE W/O DEFENSE

CUT 1 OFFENSE W/DEFENSE

2 MAN WING ENTRY DRILL

AUTOMATIC OFF W/O DEFENSE

AUTOMATIC DRILL

2 VS 1 PASSINGDRILL

2 MAN PASSING DRILL

AUTOMATIC OFFENSE

AUTOMATIC DRILL

BASELINE CUT DRILL

CUT 2 OFFENSE W/O DEFENSE

CUT 2 OFFENSE W/DEFENSE

Epilogue

"To have, give all to all"   God

This was meant to be a little book and it is. When I started it, I had in mind an essay. But, there seemed to be things that should be included and it grew too big for an essay, though I made an effort to be concise.

Also it seemed to me if I was making a case for playing in the spaces I should also give some idea of how it's done. It just so happened that I had been coaching that kind of system. I felt more comfortable suggesting to the readers something I had experience in. The result was the Monk System.

As I write this, I am not sure that anyone but me will read it. At the beginning I had thought of that and it did not deter me. I don't care. I had to write it, and it has done a lot for my growth to do so. To put these thoughts into written form in a way that others would understand them was intimidating. It forced me to think through these ideas carefully. I have gone back to films many times during the writing to confirm that what I was saying is really true. I believe it is.

In my career it has seemed to me that coaching has evolved into an ego driven profession. This is especially true since money has become such a factor. I have wondered do we coach because we love the game and the work that we do? Of course there will be denial but I still believe that there are many who love coaching and they would do it if there was very little fame or money.

What I am getting at with those questions is simply this: are we really doing any good for anyone other than ourselves? I speak for both the players and the coaches. Oh, I know the things that are done in the spotlight so people will think well of us and not as money grubbing lowlifes (NBA Cares, Read to Achieve, etc). I am not sure they should even be counted. Are they for the reason they proclaim? Or are they done as a chance to promote their name?

So I wanted to start this wrap up to the book with the quote above. It is attributed to God. Whether you believe that or not, it is a very revealing statement. It is a meaningful statement. The money conscious will think it means to give money to help people in need (this is usually more targeted for personal status than giving). I think it means more than that. Our profession is full of talented and smart people. They have something to give other than money. They have advice, mentoring, compassion, support, recommendations, time, help, and most of all helping others see the need for doing the same. I think it means giving everything that you have (not only money but skill, knowledge, experience) to all (everyone).

I have a friend who is a classical pianist. He is an outstanding pianist and teacher. He is also a man that lives for giving. He does well but is not rich. He gives of his talent. He teaches the highest level of talent, but he also teaches those that do not have that talent. He performs on the best stages, but he also performs on the small and unknown ones-many times for nothing. He gives his talent so all can hear the beautiful music he plays. He gives all, to all. He doesn't talk about it; he does it and lives it.

I feel that we all have something to give. There is nothing too small or unimportant if we are willing to give it away. It all grows.

There is a saying that I love. It is a Zen saying: "Give a man a fish and you feed him for a day. Teach him how to fish and you feed him for a lifetime." Isn't that what it's all about?

At least that's why I wrote this little book.

APPENDIX

TERMINOLOGY

In this book there may be terms that are foreign to the coach and player Some of these terms are specific to this system, and need clarification. This chapter will explain the most important ones.

SCRAMBLE

This term has been explained before in this document. I repeat it here because of its importance to our concept. Scramble occurs when organization is disrupted. This creates a situation in which players are without specific assignments and they must innovate. In scramble panic, chaos, and paralysis happen because players are not trained for these situations. The defense is especially vulnerable and it is weakest in this situation.

SPACES

Spaces are small pockets of time that take place after a structured offensive effort fails. These pockets normally occur after a fast break fails to get a shot, after a set play fails, and when a play is not used. When these conditions happen there is usually time left on the shot clock, enough time to get a good shot but not enough time for an organized attack.

LEARNED PERFORMANCE

During the initial learning process players have to think before and during a basketball activity. This is a learned performance. The activity has been taught but not repeated enough to become instinctive. It is slow, definite, and without any originality. It is robotic and predictable. It can be an individual skill (such as cutting on offense) or a team activity (running a play for example). Some players, unfortunately, do not get through the learning stage even after extensive practice and play. They are players identified as learned players, and will have difficulty playing at the pace incurred at a higher level.

INSTINCTIVE PERFORMANCE

Instinctive play is an extension of the learning stage which occurs after it is repeated until it becomes automatic. Instinctive performance uses moves, skills, adjustments, and reactions that are performed without thinking. The player functions smoothly and quickly. The learning has become internalized and the action is a process of the unconscious. Do you think about walking, eating, driving a car, riding a bicycle? You make adjustments automatically in these activities without thinking about them. In basketball this is instinctive play and it is the most effective. It is developed through extensive repetition.

RULE OFFENSE

This type of offense has no apparent structure, because it is played with the use of rules instead of specifically directed maneuvers. These rules restrict certain offensive movements, encourage some, and demand others. The rules are simple and allow freedom so the players make up, within the rules, their own play in reaction to situations. The rules are general, but cover most circumstances so that team play is not disrupted. It does not require a specific set up, though it can be used like a set play.

RULE DEFENSE

The same general explanation used in rule offense applies to defense. Team and individual defense are governed by a set of rules that apply to all situations. These rules can be used against structured offensive situations, but they also apply to freelance situations. This type of defense is invaluable in the spaces.

MONK OFFENSE

This is a rule offense. It is the core of the Monk System and can be used like a set play or in spaces. It provides a smooth transition from a failed fast break, a play breakdown, or a no-play. It is a prepared and practiced offense for unknown game situations and is required for the spaces.

SETS

Sets are a prescribed offensive system and include all types of plays: go to plays, out of bounds plays, need plays, and end of quarter plays. Zone offense is included under Sets. All of these are considered a half-court offense.

STUNTS

Some call them options, but we prefer this name because it infers deception. They basically are unpredictable choices used in the execution of various offensive maneuvers. For example, in a screen down there are five different cuts possible. Our system calls them stunts. These stunts are explained and diagramed later.

PLAY BREAKDOWN

Almost all teams run set plays but many times that play does not provide a shot and ends. This is termed a play breakdown. The time that is left is a space and the defensive team is usually in scramble. It can be difficult at times to determine if the action—such as a shot or turnover—occurs because of the play or from the breakdown. But it is important that the coach and the players understand the difference. The method for determining if points should be allocated to the play or to the breakdown has been discussed earlier.

TRANSITION

In our statistics, and in this book, Transition takes place at the end of a fast break—it is not part of it. It is like the breakdown of a play. If the Fast Break does not create a shot, but the offensive players continue to attack, it is transition. It is an extension of the fast break and very productive. Some call this a secondary fast break, but our term is consistently Transition.

NO-PLAY

There are times in a game, for whatever reason, that a play is not even attempted. For example, it may be that the team was taking advantage of a mismatch that did not work out. One situation that does occur quite often is when a team misses a shot but rebound's it and then throws it out to a teammate. The players do not set up and run a play—this would be a no-play. It is important to keep in mind this is not a breakdown, because no play was attempted.

IMPROVISATION

This is the process of invention on the spot. It is created by a player or players who don't have a specific plan because it is executed spontaneously, which makes it unpredictable. The players do not know in advance what they will do and they make things up; in reality they make their own plays at the time. To say that it is unlearned is not accurate, because with proper training, players can learn to do it instinctively and automatically. It is very effective because it is unpredictable and difficult to defend.

ABOUT THE AUTHOR

Ron Ekker has coached basketball at all levels for over 40 years. Most recently he traveled to China to start a basketball school that the National Basketball Association (NBA) sponsored. In this capacity he trained coaches and oversaw the development of young players. He has also been on the coaching staff for the Orlando Magic, Cleveland Cavaliers, and Dallas Mavericks. At the college level, he was a head coach for 15 years, NCAA Division 1 for nine of those.

Email: ekkerr748@aol.com

440-346-0037

85° 410 8161
TCN # 70CS
08 00000
0 0 0 0 5 54
463

305 762 1043